The
No Child Left Behind
Legislation:
Educational Research and
Federal Funding

A volume in
Psychological Perspectives on
Contemporary Educational Issues

Series Editors:
Jerry S. Carlson, University of California, Riverside
Joel R. Levin, University of Arizona

The
No Child Left Behind
Legislation:
Educational Research and
Federal Funding

edited by

Jerry S. Carlson

University of California, Riverside

and

Joel R. Levin

University of Arizona

INFORMATION AGE
PUBLISHING

Greenwich, Connecticut • www.infoagepub.com

0739832

Library of Congress Cataloging-in-Publication Data

The No Child Left Behind legislation:
Educational research and federal funding / edited by Jerry S.
Carlson and Joel R. Levin.
    p. cm. — (Psychological perspectives on contemporary
educational issues)
 Includes bibliographical references.
 ISBN 1-59311-187-8 (pbk.) — ISBN 1-59311-188-6 (hardcover)
 1. Education—Research—United States. 2. Education and
state—United
States. 3. Education—Research—United States—Finance. 4. United
States. No Child Left Behind Act of 2001. I. Carlson, Jerry S. II.
Levin, Joel R. III. Series.
 LB1028.25.U6S25 2005
 370'.7'2--dc22

                                                    2004028198

Printed in the United States of America

CONTENTS

FOREWORD

With the publication of this volume, *The* No Child Left Behind *Legislation: Educational Research and Federal Funding*, the scholarly journal, *Issues in Education: Contributions from Educational Psychology*, is moving to a book-series publication format. The title of this new series is *Psychological Perspectives on Contemporary Educational Issues* and, in the capable hands of George Johnson, the spirit of *Issues* will continue to be published by Information Age Publishing in Greenwich, Connecticut.

NEW FORMAT

Issues was first published in 1995 and has appeared twice yearly since. *Issues'* dual purpose was to: (1) identify significant issues in education; and (2) address them through the lenses of educational psychology, psychology, and related disciplines. Topics selected for analysis were broad in scope and of relevance to a wide audience of researchers and practitioners concerned with critical educational problems. Each issue of *Issues* featured a single focus article, followed by a number of critiques or commentaries. These were responded to by the focus article author(s) in a "final word." In addition to the invited focus articles and critiques, *Issues* featured a review essay of a book or books addressing a topic of importance in education. The founding editor of the journal was Jerry Carlson. Robert Calfee served as the book review editor. Since 2001, Jerry Carlson has co-edited the journal with Joel Levin, with Robert Calfee continuing as book review editor. The editorial board has included Steven Asher, Sam Ball, Virginia Berninger, Peter Bryant, J. P. Das, Earl Hunt, Richard Mayer, Angela O'Donnell, Michael Pressley, Leona Schauble, Wolfgang Schneider, and David Wood.

Now, to facilitate distribution of *Issues* and to serve interested readers better, it is important to change the publishing format of the journal to a book series. But, importantly, the purpose of the series will be consistent with *Issues in Education: Contributions from Educational Psychology*. The topics selected for inclusion will continue to be relevant and important to a wide audience and the authors invited to participate will continue to be carefully chosen. Be assured, however, that the change in publishing format will not affect or diminish in any way the standards and high quality that readers have come to expect of *Issues*. The editors of *Psychological Perspectives on Contemporary Educational Issues* look forward to our exciting new adventure, beginning with this initial volume.

So, welcome aboard to a volume highlighting a provocative focal article on issues associated with federally funded, scientifically-based education research by Valerie Reyna, the former senior research advisor of the Institute of Education Sciences (IES), with commentaries by a varied group of distinguished responders!

Jerry S. Carlson and Joel R. Levin
Editors

Past volumes of *Issues in Education*

CHAPTER 1

THE *NO CHILD LEFT BEHIND ACT* AND SCIENTIFIC RESEARCH

A View from Washington, DC

Valerie F. Reyna

Three days after taking office in January 2001 as the 43rd President of the United States, George W. Bush announced proposals for educational reform that he described as "the cornerstone of my Administration." Both the *No Child Left Behind Act* and the *Education Sciences Reform Act* were subsequently signed into law. In this chapter, I discuss the implications of this historic legislation for educational research. In particular, I draw on my experience in Washington, D.C., with these initiatives as a senior advisor in the U.S. Department of Education and, more importantly, as a scientist who has published on a variety of topics in learning and memory.

The No Child Left Behind *Legislation:*
Educational Research and Federal Funding, 1–25
Copyright © 2005 by Information Age Publishing
All rights of reproduction in any form reserved.

BACKGROUND

Despite the terrorist attacks on September 11, 2001 and a national economic downturn, the *No Child Left Behind Act* was signed into law on January 8, 2002 with broad bipartisan congressional support. With less fanfare, the *Education Sciences Reform Act* was signed into law on November 5, 2002 to establish a new federal research agency, capping a 2-year effort to ensure that educational practices in the United States are based on sound scientific evidence. The phrase "scientifically based research" is mentioned more than 110 times in the *No Child Left Behind Act* and, naturally, is the raison d'être behind the establishment of the research agency, the Institute of Education Sciences, that supports the gathering of statistical, evaluation, and research data relevant to education. Although I cannot cover all of the intricacies of these pieces of legislation in this chapter (the full texts can be accessed via the Web at http://www.ed.gov/legislation/ESEA02/ and http://www.ed.gov/legislation/EdSciencesRef/, respectively), I will review definitions of scientific research offered in the legislation, domains of educational practice that are now mandated to be based on scientific research, and the implications of these mandates for the nature of educational research and the training of educational professionals. The main conclusion that emerges from this analysis is that if this legislation is to be successful, fundamental changes must be made in the kind of educational research that is conducted and in how colleges and universities prepare prospective researchers, practitioners, policymakers, and other educational decision makers.

OVERVIEW OF SOME CONCERNS THAT OTIVATED THE LEGISLATION

The concerns that I now discuss are documented in press releases from the U.S. Department of Education, public statements by officials of both the legislative and executive branches, and in numerous internal and external communications. For example, Figures 1.1 through 1.4 display the dismally low levels of educational achievement as measured by the National Assessment of Educational Progress (and increasing expenditures) that antedated the *No Child Left Behind* legislation. In Figure 1.1, reading achievement among fourth graders (a meager 32% are proficient) is plotted against federal spending, and shows little improvement despite increases in federal spending (see also Figure 1.2). Figures 1.3 and 1.4 provide snapshots of even lower achievement levels in mathematics and science among 12th graders. Figure 1.5 breaks out achievement in mathematics and reading by ethnic group, revealing still lower performance

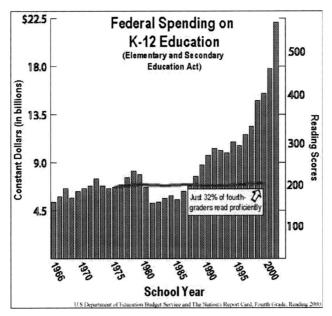

Figure 1.1.   Federal spending on K-12 Education, U.S. Department of Education Budget Service and National Center for Education Statistics.

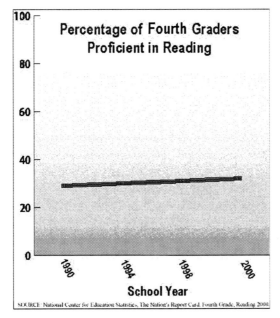

Figure 1.2.   Percentage of fourth graders proficient in reading, National Center for Education Statistics

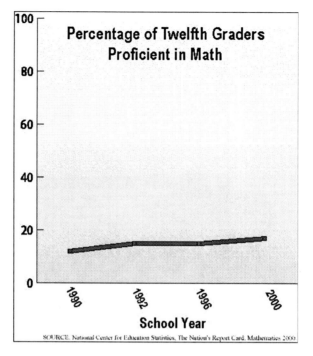

Figure 1.3. Percentage of 12th graders proficient in
mathematics, National Center for Education Statistics

among a heretofore "invisible" minority, Hispanics. Against this depress-
ing backdrop of low achievement, the stage was set for legislation that
promised a new approach.

Some of the philosophical assumptions that motivated the legislation
include the belief that current levels of academic achievement are unac-
ceptably low, that low achievement threatens our national economic com-
petitiveness, that almost all children (save those with profound cognitive
disabilities) can learn, and that disparities in achievement across racial,
ethnic, and socioeconomic groups are offensive to the American ethos of
equal opportunity and impractical in the light of changing demographics.
The nation will increasingly depend on women and minorities to fill crucial roles in the economy, and the lower achievement of these groups
(especially in science and technology) places the nation at risk. A corollary
of the latter view is that disparities in educational outcomes across groups
should not be papered over with summary statistics (Figure 1.5). The status quo of low achievement can be changed, it is argued, by basing educational practices on scientific research demonstrating effectiveness of those

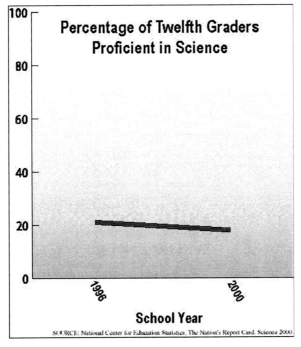

Figure 1.4.   Percentage of 12th graders proficient in
science, National Center for Education Statistics

practices, assessing academic achievement reliably, and holding educators
accountable for results.

This thinking about accountability fits a triage model, which is implied
in the title of the legislation *No Child Left Behind*, as contrasted with a metaphor of getting ahead or being first in the world in educational achievement. (The word *triage* in emergency medicine refers to the practice of
prioritizing treatment so that patients who are most badly injured or ill,
or whose situation is most critical, are stabilized first.) I should hasten to
add that the legislation mentions and supports leading the world in education (e.g., providing financial incentives to encourage more students to
take Advanced Placement courses), but the dominant metaphor involves
shoring up achievement levels of the lowest achieving students to ensure a
minimum acceptable level of reading and other basic skills. The logic is
that resources are limited and should be assigned first to basic needs, and
second to anything else. Once basic verbal and quantitative skills have
been mastered (as well as content knowledge in domains such as history
and science), students have the means to learn other material. Without
basic skills, however, students are trapped, unable to read to learn as

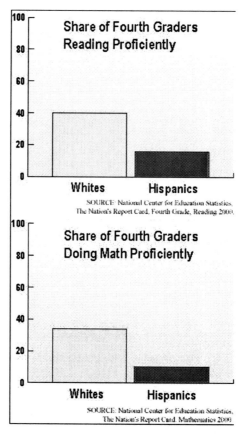

Figure 1.5.   Percentage of White and Hispanic fourth graders proficient in reading (Panel A) and in mathematics (Panel B), National Center for Education Statistics

opposed to learn to read. A key assumption is that schools that excel well beyond minimum standards do not have to be concerned about assessments of basic skills; such advanced students should easily pass basic skills tests. (The issues of which tests, how many tests, and their lengths should be separated from the core issue of accountability in principle.) Hence, concerns that high-achieving schools will abandon challenging curricula in order to "teach to the test" seem ill-founded: Over-preparing for tests unnecessarily or administering invalid tests are not a consequence of what is in the legislation but are examples of poor implementation of sound principles. Therefore, supporters of the legislation maintain that if tests assess basic skills and students have not mastered such skills to an acceptable level of proficiency, teaching to a reliable and valid test of necessary skills is desirable.

A theme that permeates both sets of legislation, *No Child Left Behind* and the *Education Sciences Reform Act*, is the need for greater emphasis on *learning*, not to the exclusion of other important educational outcomes but as the central goal of education. For example, the importance of promoting social and emotional development in preschool programs is openly acknowledged in the legislation, but the need to adequately prepare children for school during those crucial preschool years is emphasized. The assumption is that children will be emotionally healthier if they are successful academically, all other factors being equal, and that this can be accomplished in a supportive and nurturing environment. Although it seems illogical, much of the research supported by the U.S. Department of Education heretofore has not focused on learning as a primary objective. Psychology departments, rather than Colleges of Education, and agencies other than those in Education, have been the sources of much of the scientific evidence on learning and cognition relevant to education over the last several decades. (Readers should note that there are outstanding exceptions to this gross generalization.) Whether this trend will change as a result of the new legislation is debatable, but the need for interdisciplinary collaboration to address issues such as mathematics learning is straightforward; research has shown that better content knowledge of the disciplines in science and mathematics is associated with higher student achievement. Parents, students, and school personnel are unlikely to care whether the scientists who help students achieve adequate yearly progress are classified as psychologists, economists, mathematicians, sociologists, or belong to some other discipline: The plural usage "education sciences" was intentional. Indeed, parochial concerns such as how much money has been "set aside" for researchers in Colleges of Education or for a specific type of research (e.g. qualitative research) regardless of the merit of individual proposals, will increasingly marginalize their proponents.

Thus, the four pillars of the *No Child Left Behind Act* are (1) accountability for results, (2) tempered by flexibility and local control, (3) increases in choices available to parents of students attending Title I schools that fail to meet State standards, and (4) an emphasis on educational programs and practices that have been clearly demonstrated to be effective through rigorous scientific research. The main components of the *Education Sciences Reform Act* are the replacement of the Office of Educational Research and Improvement with the Institute of Education Sciences, appointment of a director to serve a 6-year term (as opposed to terms tied to the coming and going of the administration), and the establishment of three divisions: the National Center for Education Research, the National Center for Education Statistics (reaffirming the old NCES), and the National Center for Education Evaluation and Regional Assistance. Two major changes that preceded the creation of the Institute of Education Sciences, but were carried over, were the development of peer-review policies that more closely resemble those of other scientific research agencies and the transfer of substantial evaluation activities from other entities in the Department of Education to the research agency.

Enormously influential, the National Academy of Science's Committee on Scientific Principles for Education Research laid the groundwork for many of the aforementioned changes (Shavelson & Towne, 2002). Manuscripts of the Committee's report, and later the final published product, circulated during the period that legislation was under consideration, and dog-eared copies could be spied in the hands of key Congressional staffers and administration officials. The Committee concluded that educational research is subject to the same scientific methods as other fields, and delineated the diverse approaches common to science. Sensibly, the Committee noted that methods should fit the questions posed in research: Descriptive research, based on objective measures, requires different methods than research seeking to establish cause-and-effect relationships. Cause-and-effect questions require random assignment (whether comparisons are between or within subjects), which is, therefore, the gold standard for evaluating "what works." However, other kinds of data can narrow down hypotheses about what works, and what works is not the only important scientific question. Questions of mechanism—how a practice or program works—are a neglected area of research and are essential for generalizing proven practices to different contexts and populations (Reyna, 2004). Experimental designs are frequently used to test hypotheses about mechanism (see Bjorklund, 1995; Schwartz & Reisberg, 1991; Siegler, 1991). The Committee also made recommendations about research policy, pointing out that qualified researchers were necessary to staff, at least in part, a credible research agency. The Committee's efforts are currently being followed up by a distinguished panel of scholars under the leadership of the National Academy of Sciences. The Strategic Educational Research Partnership, or SERP, is also currently formulating recommendations for research in education. The President of the National Academy of Sciences has placed education at the forefront of concerns for this august body, and its formal involvement is maintained in the *Education Sciences Reform Act*.

The What Works Clearinghouse is another project that spanned the prelegislative and postlegislative periods (wwcinfo@w-w-c.org), both influencing and being influenced by the legislation. Building on the rationale for the Campbell Collaboration in the social sciences, which was, in turn, modeled on the Cochran Collaboration in medicine, the What Works Clearinghouse was intended to provide scientifically sound and independent reviews of practices and programs in education in a user-friendly format (Mosteller & Boruch, 2002). The Statement of Work soliciting competitive bids for the contract to implement a What Works Clearing-house underwent numerous revisions to balance concerns about quality control and rigor with transparency and independence. The selection of a contract mechanism to accomplish this task indicates that the federal government, in this case the Institute of Education Sciences, will continue to exert control over the Clearinghouse. The primary contractors for the What Works Clearinghouse are the American Institutes for Research and the Campbell Collaboration, and include subcontractors such as Aspen Systems, Caliber Associates, and the Education Quality Institute (another organization, along with the Coalition for Evidence-Based Policy, that played a role in the impetus for evidence-based practice). At this time, the What Works Clearinghouse has completed the solicitation of public comment about procedures for applying scientific standards to evidence of effectiveness; procedures for adjudicating among claims of effectiveness are forthcoming.

Guiding the What Works Clearinghouse is a Technical Advisory Group consisting of social science methodologists with:

- Significant track records of peer-reviewed publications in high-quality journals
- Demonstrated proficiency in conducting and publishing empirical research
- Particular expertise in experimental and quasi-experimental designs, tests and measurements, and research syntheses

If education is to be based on evidence, such expertise is necessary (but not sufficient) for *any major policy recommendation* or any decision to adopt particular practices or programs.

SCIENTIFIC RESEARCH IN THE *NO CHILD LEFT BEHIND ACT*

Under section 9101 of General Provisions of the *No Child Left Behind Act*, the definition of scientifically based research is given as follows:
Except as otherwise provided, in this Act:

(37) SCIENTIFICALLY BASED RESEARCH—The term "scientifically based research"

(A) means research that involves the application of rigorous, systematic, and objective procedures to obtain reliable and valid knowledge relevant to education activities and programs; and

(B)   includes research that

> (i)   employs systematic, empirical methods that draw on observation or experiment;
>
> (ii) involves rigorous data analyses that are adequate to test the stated hypotheses and justify the general conclusions drawn;
>
> (iii) relies on measurements or observational methods that provide reliable and valid data across evaluators and observers, across multiple measurements and observations, and across studies by the same or different investigators;
>
> (iv) is evaluated using experimental or quasi-experimental designs in which individuals, entities, programs, or activities are assigned to different conditions and with appropriate controls to evaluate the effects of the condition of interest, with a preference for random-assignment experiments, or other designs to the extent that those designs contain within-condition or across-condition controls;
>
> (v)   ensures that experimental studies are presented in sufficient detail and clarity to allow for replication or, at a minimum, offer the opportunity to build systematically on their findings; and
>
> (vi) has been accepted by a peer-reviewed journal or approved by a panel of independent experts through a comparably rigorous, objective, and scientific review.

Scientists will recognize familiar notions of objective empirical observations, valid and reliable measures, appropriate experimental designs and controls, analyses that test hypotheses, replicability, and peer review. Although these methods have been available for centuries, and have been applied successfully to human learning (Schwartz & Reisberg, 1991), they have not been used consistently to inform educational practice. This has occurred despite worked examples being applied to educational research (Campbell & Stanley, 1963; Cronbach, 1982) and cogent appeals to educational researchers to enhance the credibility and impact of their work (Levin & O'Donnell, 1999).

Although professional wisdom will remain the source of many judgments about effective programs and practices simply because relevant evidence is unavailable, the onus is now on practitioners and other decision makers to use teaching methods with demonstrated effectiveness. Just as it is unimaginable to administer untested drugs to patients or, worse, to fail to administer proven lifesaving treatments in favor of unproven ones, so it should become unimaginable to forego proven methods in education.

The *No Child Left Behind Act* does not rely on the discretion of researchers or educators but, rather, mandates the use of scientific research in various areas. In addition to the general provision to base practice on scientific research, as stated above, individual sections concerning a range of programs also mandate its use. For example, Title I assistance programs are *required* to use instructional strategies grounded in scientific research. School improvement plans, professional development, and technical assistance that districts provide to low-performing schools must also be based on strategies that have been proven to be effective.

More specifically,

- States must assist school districts in developing or identifying high-quality, effective curricula aligned with state academic achievement standards, and must disseminate such curricula to each district and school within the state.

- School districts are required to take into account the experience of model programs for the educationally disadvantaged and the findings of relevant scientifically based research as they develop their plans for services.

- Both school-wide and targeted assistance programs are required to use effective instructional methods and strategies based on scientifically based research.

- Schools identified for improvement must develop 2-year improvement plans that incorporate strategies based on scientifically based research. School districts must provide technical assistance to these schools, such as identifying and implementing professional development, instructional strategies, and methods of instruction that are grounded in scientifically based research and have been proven effective in addressing the specific instructional issues that caused the school to be identified.

- School districts identified for improvement must incorporate scientifically based research strategies in their improvement plans. State technical assistance to identified school districts must be based on scientifically based research.

- If a school district is identified for corrective action and a new curriculum is implemented, the state must provide professional development based on scientifically based research.

- School support teams, whose top priority is to provide assistance to schools subject to corrective action, are to be composed of persons who are knowledgeable about scientifically based research and practice on teaching and learning, as well as about successful schoolwide projects, school reform, and improving educational opportunities for low-achieving students (*No Child Left Behind: A Desktop Reference*, http://www.ed.gov/admins/lead/account/nclbreference/index.html?src=mr).

The Comprehensive School Reform (CSR) program builds on the Title I schoolwide program by providing greater flexibility in the use of federal funds and by encouraging the implementation of effective strategies for all students in a school. The CSR program gives financial assistance to schools in order to implement whole school reforms that reflect research on effective practices, helping students meet state academic standards. Grantees *must* rely on scientifically proven strategies; each CSR plan *must* include scientifically proven teaching and learning strategies.

Similar mandates are outlined for reading. *Reading First* is a formula grant program to states based on the number of students ages 5 to 17 below the poverty line. States receiving grant awards from the U.S. Department of Education then make competitive grants to school districts. States must develop plans to assist districts in using "scientifically based" reading research to improve reading instruction and raise student achievement. The goal of *Reading First* is to ensure that every child can read at grade level (or higher) by the end of third grade through the implementation of instructional programs and materials, assessments, and professional development grounded in scientific reading research. More specifically,

- State education agencies or school districts must select professional development, instructional programs, and materials that focus on the five key areas that scientific reading research has identified as essential components of reading instruction: phonemic awareness, phonics, vocabulary, fluency, and reading comprehension.
- *Reading First* provides increased teacher professional development to ensure that teachers are able to teach scientifically based instructional programs.

The new *Early Reading First Program* extends the goals of *Reading First* to younger learners. It is a federally administered discretionary grant program in which the U.S. Department of Education makes competitive awards for up to 3 years to local school districts, other public or private organizations, or collaborations. These organizations apply for awards on behalf of preschool programs to strengthen the literacy components of early childhood centers. Grantees must use *Early Reading First* funds to provide preschoolers with high-quality oral language and literature-rich environments; provide professional development to staff based on scientific research about methods that enhance linguistic and cognitive skills;

and provide activities and instructional materials that are grounded in scientifically based reading research.

In some instances, pre-existing programs were retained in the legislation but strengthened through mandates involving research. For example, the *Even Start Family Literacy Program* provides low-income families with integrated literacy services for parents and their young children (birth through age 7). *Even Start* is primarily a state-administered discretionary grant program in which states hold competitions to award subgrants to partnerships of local school districts and other organizations. *Even Start* programs have new requirements under *No Child Left Behind* to use scientifically based research evidence to design program activities, especially reading-readiness activities for preschool children.

Many of the programs in the legislation address the means by which skills and knowledge are attained, rather than the skills themselves. For example, educational technologies have proliferated in schools despite their expense, rapid obsolescence, and outstandingly poor record of inspiring competent scientific research on effectiveness in promoting learning (Reyna, Brainerd, Effken, Bootzin, & Lloyd, 2001). The legislation is aimed at improving this state of affairs by emphasizing the "implementation of proven strategies" and by requiring districts to base the strategies they use for integrating technology into curricula and instruction on reviews of relevant research. Specifically, the goals of the Educational Technology State Grants Program are to improve learning through the use of technology in elementary and secondary schools and to assist every student in becoming technologically literate by the end of eighth grade. These goals will be achieved, it is hoped, by integrating technology resources and systems with teacher training and professional development to establish research-based instructional models. The program targets funds primarily to school districts that serve poor students.

Other programs address research-based teacher training and development as a means of achieving better learning. These programs include *Early Childhood Educator Professional Development, Teaching American History, Improving Teacher Quality State Grants*, and the *Mathematics and Science Partnerships*. The *Early Childhood Educator Professional Development* program funds partnerships whose goal is to improve the knowledge and skills of early childhood educators who work in mainly low socioeconomic areas by basing professional development on scientific research and training those professionals to apply the best available research on early childhood pedagogy, child development, and learning. The *Teaching American History* program aims to increase students' knowledge of history by providing funds to school districts to design, implement, and demonstrate effective, research-based professional development programs. The *Improving Teacher Quality State Grants* program also stipulates the use of scientifically based professional development interventions. All activities supported with Title II funds must be based on a review of scientifically based research that shows how such interventions are expected to improve student achievement. As the *Desktop Reference* helpfully notes,

> For example, if a state decides to fund interventions such as professional development in math, the state must be able to show how the particular activities are grounded in a review of activities that have been correlated with increases in student achievement. (p. 58)

Finally, the *Mathematics and Science Partnerships* program is a discretionary grant program that supports enhanced training and recruitment of high-quality math and science teachers. Grants are targeted to partnerships of high-need school districts and to science, mathematics, and engineering schools within universities, giving districts and universities joint responsibility for educating teachers. (Note that cognitive scientists—experts on student learning—are not mandated partners, but learning experts could help teachers more effectively transmit science content.) In years that the program receives more than $100 million, the U.S. Department of Education will allocate funds to states by formula so that they can award subgrants to partnerships of institutions of higher education and high-need local education agencies. Grants are awarded for 3 years and grantees must:

- Institute reforms that are aligned with academic standards in mathematics and science.
- Engage in teacher training and learning activities that are based on scientific research.

The language of the section on *Mathematics and Science Partnerships* emphasizes the use of high-quality, research-based practices in instruction. Partnerships are authorized to conduct only those training activities that are based on scientific research. Whether this is construed as training that is broadly commensurate with research or for which formal evaluations have been conducted of specific programs remains to be seen.

Addressing learning and teacher training, the section on limited English proficiency reiterates some of the features of the broad definition of "scientifically based research" in the General Provisions. Foremost, language instruction curricula used to teach limited English proficient children must be tied to scientifically based research and demonstrated to be effective. (The Institute of Education Sciences convened an expert panel of empirical scientists to review this literature, the National Literacy Panel on Language Minority Children and Youth; their preliminary report is expected in 2004.) School districts must use Title III funds to provide high-quality language instruction programs that are based on scientific research, and that have demonstrated effectiveness in both improving English proficiency and student achievement. State education agencies have similar constraints. In addition, professional development must be informed by scientifically based research that demonstrates its effectiveness in increasing children's English proficiency or teachers' knowledge and skills.

Given the increased emphasis on students with limited English proficiency in many quarters, it is useful to note that specific language concerning multiple approaches to research is included in section 3222 of the legislation. That is,

(a) ADMINISTRATION—The Secretary shall conduct research activities authorized by this subpart through the Office of Educational Research and Improvement in coordination and collaboration with the Office of English Language Acquisition, Language Enhancement, and Academic Achievement for Limited English Proficient Students.

(b) REQUIREMENTS—Such research activities
    (1) shall have a practical application to teachers, counselors, paraprofessionals, school administrators, parents, and others involved in improving the education of limited English proficient children and their families;
    (2) may include research on effective instruction practices for multilingual classes, and on effective instruction strategies to be used by a teacher or other staff member who does not know the native language of a limited English proficient child in the teacher's or staff member's classroom;
    (3) may include establishing (through the National Center for Education Statistics in consultation with experts in second language acquisition and scientifically based research on teaching limited English proficient children) a common definition of limited English proficient children for purposes of national data collection; and
    (4) shall be administered by individuals with expertise in second language acquisition, scientifically based research on teaching limited English proficient children, and the needs of limited English proficient children and their families.

(c) FIELD-INITIATED RESEARCH—
    (1) IN GENERAL—The Secretary shall reserve not less than 5% of the funds made available to carry out this section for field-initiated research conducted by recipients of grants under

subpart 1 or this subpart who have received such grants within the previous 5 years. Such research may provide for longitudinal studies of limited English proficient children or teachers who serve such children, monitoring the education of such children from entry into language instruction educational programs through secondary school completion.

(d) CONSULTATION—The Secretary shall consult with agencies, organizations, and individuals that are engaged in research and practice on the education of limited English proficient children, language instruction educational programs, or related research, to identify areas of study and activities to be funded under this section.

(e) (e) DATA COLLECTION—The Secretary shall provide for the collection of data on limited English proficient children as part of the data systems operated by the Department.

Last in this nonexhaustive review of programs that explicitly mention the use of scientific research is a program that does not directly address the acquisition of skills or the inculcation of training, the *Dropout Prevention Program*. The program is primarily a grant program to state education agencies and local school districts to implement research-based, sustainable, and coordinated school dropout prevention and reentry programs. As the researchers who spoke at the White House Conference on Character and Community on June 19, 2002 (http://www.ed.gov/inits/character/) pointed out, there is a nascent body of scientific evidence indicating that prosocial behavior can be fostered by school-based programs, and that important outcomes such as reductions in dropping out and drug use can be achieved using scientifically tested interventions.

IMPLICATIONS FOR EDUCATIONAL RESEARCH AND THE TRAINING OF EDUCATIONAL PROFESSIONALS

Other writers have presaged many of the implications of the *No Child Left Behind Act* and the *Education Science Reform Act* for the nature of research, and I will not attempt to recapitulate them here (e.g., Levin & O'Donnell, 1999; Shavelson & Towne, 2002; Slavin, in press). The bottom line of both pieces of legislation is that research in education must now satisfy the canons of science, just as scientific research in other fields has done for some time (guidelines in Campbell & Stanley, 1963, and Cronbach, 1982, remain timely). The *No Child Left Behind Act* mandates determining what educational programs and practices have been clearly demonstrated to be effective through rigorous scientific research. Federal funding will then be targeted to support the programs and teaching methods that improve student learning and achievement. How broadly these strictures are interpreted remains to be seen. However, it seems inevitable that the standards for research in education have begun to move upward, and practitioners and decision makers who adhere to high scientific standards will find that their programs and practices satisfy the law. Although there may be some programs and practices that slip by for which evidence is weak or nonexistent, the appetite for science will expand in the next decades for several reasons.

First, as more teachers, administrators, and policy makers become educated about the scientific method, they will become more skeptical consumers. Less snake oil will be sold and more real medicine will become available. As has happened in other fields when the flow of research information is facilitated and disputants accept that scientific evidence will be used to settle disputes, the good will drive out the bad. Signals of this attitude change in the schools include a far more receptive response to the use of random assignment to groups in school-based research. Only a year ago, it would have been accurate to assert that schools were philosophically opposed to "experimenting" with their students (see Reyna, in press). Today, although still a minority attitude but one that is rapidly changing, more school personnel understand the rationale behind random assignment and recognize that, for important decisions about instructional programs or practices, random assignment to groups is essential for finding out what works. Rather than being unethical, in fact, experiments are the ethical choice for responsible educators who realize that they have an obligation to find out what works for the sake of the students.

Education faces a special challenge with respect to accepting scientific evidence as the basis for settling disputes. Educational researchers have often stooped to ad hominem personal attack in lieu of data, impugning the motives of those who disagree with them. The public and educators must learn to vehemently reject this form of argumentation. Journalists must begin to ask invariably after every claim about educational mechanisms or effectiveness, what is the evidence for that conclusion? Because of the importance of journalism ("the press") in our constitution and in societal progress, all reporters must become science reporters to the extent that they understand the basics of scientific methods and can ask nongullible questions of advocates espousing particular programs or educational approaches. (If such advocates are mistaken, their programs and approaches are not innocuous; they threaten the well being of the nation's children.) Schools of journalism should provide adequate preparation through coursework that exposes students to scientific methods and scientific skepticism, and through apprenticeships with empirical scientists during the training process. Much nonsense and damage could be avoided with savvy reporting.

It is well known from psychological research that negative information has a greater impact than otherwise comparable positive information (e.g., Nisbett & Ross, 1980). Science provides a practiced self-discipline in reining in such normal human reactions: We must accept that people with disagreeable motives can be correct just as those we admire can be wrong. We must accept that intuitive plausibility is not the same as evidence. The facts care little about how beautiful, compelling, or coherent our stories are or whether the scientist in question is a likeable person. Moreover, critical thinking must be applied to all educational claims. It is perhaps an indictment of our educational system that much of the debate in the pages of educational magazines and journals would not pass muster as "critical thinking" (see Halpern, 2003, for definitions and research on critical thinking). For example, a vocal minority has cast aspersions on one of the few comprehensive school reform programs with respectable scientific evidence indicating positive outcomes. *Success for All* is impugned as *Success for Some*, with much winking and nodding about how researchers have characterized their data. Unfortunately, the price of success in educational research is too often unsubstantiated attacks. However, it should be clear that no educational program is expected to achieve absolute 100% success and that the title conveys an ideal. Indeed, the researchers report less than perfect results. Why would such an aspersion have any appeal to a reasonably intelligent audience (it has been passed on with little critical comment in respectable outlets such as the *Washington Post*)? Similarly, I have heard educators and researchers debate whether a program should be described as "effective" because it is not equally effective with every student. Antibiotics are not 100% effective with every patient, and yet no one is seriously advocating that we should discourage their use when indicated or that they be considered ineffective because they fail to achieve "success for all." It seems that only in education would such ludicrous arguments be taken seriously.

Second, as the word gets out that there are superior instructional methods that are more likely to produce learning, educators will clamor to have access to the methods that yield "adequate yearly progress" as opposed to frustration, disappointment, and loss of federal funding. Funds will be increasingly directed to after-school and other programs that have been scientifically demonstrated to prevent drug use and violence among youths. As students, parents, and educators experience these outcomes, they will work to maintain and enhance them. The key to achieving these consequences of pressure to maintain effective programs, naturally, is that Congress and the administration must hold fast to their resolve to avoid fatal compromises that lower the standards for account-ability.

Such experience with positive outcomes has characterized early read-ing interventions, which have been shown to reduce reading disabilities and, consequently, the need for costly special education. Early reading research has been a scientific success story that has inspired new requests for proposals for research in reading comprehension, mathematics learn-ing, teacher quality and other areas where more research is needed. In addition, there is widespread acknowledgment that, as noted in the description of the Cognition and Student Learning Program of the Insti-tute of Education Sciences, "the most important outcome of education is student learning." The description goes on: "In order for students to suc-ceed in school, they must attend to, remember, and reason effectively about information, whether that information is provided by teachers, textbooks, or via computers. These three components of cognition are the basis for achievement in reading, science, mathematics, and other school subjects." Because it encompasses the encoding, processing, and learning of information, *cognition is the basic science of education*. Thus, all educa-tional professionals should be thoroughly conversant with research on how students attend to, remember, and reason about information.

Specifically, in order to be relevant to the practice of education under the new legislation, teacher-training programs should inculcate deep con-ceptual understanding of rigorous research on cognition and, for those who teach younger learners, on developmental differences in cognition. Topics in basic (attention, memory, and perception) and higher-order (reasoning, problem solving, and decision making) cognition are a must, and would include:

> attention; working memory; learning processes (acquisition and retention); storage in and retrieval from long-term memory; interference and inhibi-tion; executive function and monitoring; metamemory or memory strate-gies; meaning extraction (literal and figurative) for words, sentences, and discourse; inference and critical thinking (semantic, logical, and pragmatic inferences, situation models, and other mental representations); similarity, categorization, and analogical reasoning; non-verbal reasoning (e.g., spatial, scientific, and quantitative reasoning); domain-specific knowledge (e.g., biology, calculus, or American history) and conceptual development; and judgment and decision-making. (Cognition and Student Learning program)

Training for leadership or policy-making positions should also include these topics as fundamental to understanding student learning. Con-versely, those who lacked this crucial knowledge would not be adequately prepared to make decisions about instructional approaches, textbook adoption, or other policies or practices intended to produce learning. In addition, an intensive course or courses in statistics, assessment, research design, and methodology should be mandatory for teachers, leaders, and, ideally, policy makers. No one should graduate from a bona fide college or university with a degree in education who does not know what a valid and reliable test is, and how that is judged. These topics are not the only subjects that educators should know about, but their importance is much greater given the new legislation. The topics have been successfully taught to these populations in the past, so arguments about feasibility ignore the fact that this has already been accomplished, albeit not equally well everywhere. Teaching important material well, however, ought to be the business of education.

As this discussion implies, many Colleges of Education will have to make changes to remain relevant to educational practice in the twenty-first century. Presidents and provosts of institutions of higher education should immediately assess whether their deans are knowledgeable and comfortable with scientific approaches to education. Those who are not comfortable with science are analogous to the buggy whip makers of the latter century at the dawn of the era of the automobile. It is often remarked that change in higher education occurs slowly. Few central administrators are acting on the realization that the train is moving rapidly forward without the deans and faculty of many Colleges of Education on board. A conversation with a respected president of a Research I university (a classification indicating a major research institution) illustrates the disconnect that is widely evident: In discussing potential candidates for a deanship of his College of Education, the president remarked that he was leery of hiring an outstanding researcher because of his concern about being relevant to what really happens in schools, implying that research and practice were somehow antithetical. As the review of the new legislation indicates, high levels of research competence must now be viewed as minimum qualifications to be relevant to educational practice in schools. The changes made to the *Elementary and Secondary Education Act* as reauthorized by the *No Child Left Behind* legislation are a challenge, and they present numerous problems of appropriate implementation that would benefit from the dedication and experience of members of Colleges of Education. The changes are also an unprecedented opportunity to make progress on behalf of students and be central to a top national concern. Because of the emphasis on research in the legislation, colleges and universities can be more important than they have ever been in educational practice—if they rise to the challenge and respond.

POSTSCRIPT: PROMISING OPPORTUNITIES, LOOMING OBSTACLES

Research has been published that fits the model I have described, research that is rigorous, theoretically informed, and useful in the classroom (e.g., in mathematics learning, Ashcraft & Kirk, 2001; Carpenter, Fennema, Peterson, Chiang, & Loef, 1989; Nye, Hedges, Konstantopoulos; 2001; Siegler, 1988). These and many other studies provide a solid foundation for future work, including new research programs initiated under the aegis of *No Child Left Behind* and the *Education Sciences Reform Act* (see also the American Psychological Society *Observer*, 2003). One project, for example, infuses a Web-based science curriculum for middle and high school students with "desirable difficulties," counterintuitive ways of improving learning to maximize long-term retention. These desirable difficulties include spacing rather than massing study sessions, reducing feedback, and using tests as learning interventions. Intuitive plausibility would deliver a "thumbs down" for most of these interventions, and, yet, the evidence indicates that they have the potential to revolutionize the efficiency of learning. An educational researcher (Marcia Linn), who has worked in the "trenches" in schools, and a cognitive psychologist (Robert Bjork), who was inspired to translate basic research into practice, joined forces on this project to improve education. Sustained and sufficient funding is necessary to build a critical mass of such researchers, innovative and willing to tackle educationally significant issues. Although some think of educationally relevant research as mainly random-assignment evaluation studies that can be churned out formulaically with assured payoffs, it is crucial to focus the attention of the nation's best minds on educational problems. The best minds will not be drawn to doing unimaginative "piece work" performed at the government's behest. Furthermore, although formulaic evaluation can be highly useful, it is not the source of new ideas. Without innovative research, there will eventually be little to evaluate. Strictly basic research cannot be counted on to develop in the direction of educationally significant issues. For evidence-based education to become a reality, relevant research must be nurtured at each point along the continuum from basic to applied science, with improving learning the ultimate goal.

It should be noted that a major factor that will affect efficient progress toward evidence-based education is human-subjects regulations. Human-subjects regulations could be the undoing of the progress toward science enshrined in the *No Child Left Behind Act*. Because of what seems to be a sincere desire to protect human subjects, but without any realistic cost-benefit analysis of the burdens of regulations, regulations under consideration at this time may present an unreasonable burden to researchers.

Regulations may become so onerous that many researchers, especially good ones, will refuse to conduct research in schools. According to the legislation, this would be a problem because conducting school-based research is in the national interest. On the one hand, most behavioral science research that is confidential and anonymous does not place subjects at greater risk than normal activities of living, but is nevertheless subjected to levels of bureaucracy that are incommensurate with its potential risk at great expense to the nation. Ironically, the ethics of such practices have been increasingly questioned. On the other hand, researchers must become more sensitive to valid concerns about privacy and interference with relationships within families, as expressed by members of Congress and others. For example, parents certainly have a right to prevent the solicitation of personal family information from their minor children. The use of informed parental consent, which is current practice, along with technology that strips personal identifiers from data but allows researchers to connect data records from the same individual may hold the key to rational compromise on this issue.

CONCLUSIONS

Scientists and policy makers have come to Washington in the past, worked very hard, and have had relatively little success in passing legislation or raising standards for educational research. (As with every statement I have made in this chapter, there are notable exceptions to this conclusion.) Within a short window of time, in contrast, spanning roughly the spring of 2001 to the fall of 2002, two landmark pieces of legislation were passed that could substantially change educational practice in the nation for the better. The most important aspect of this legislation was not any specific program or policy but, rather, the wholesale embrace of the scientific method for generating knowledge that will govern educational practice in classrooms across the nation. Scientific evidence is not sufficient to decide practice; human values and other considerations are also important. However, evidence is a necessary precursor to responsible decision making about issues that affect students' lives. Furthermore, because scientific hypotheses (e.g., about what works or how it works) are subject to empirical challenges, science is self-correcting. As inconsistencies develop, the conventional wisdom of the day (even when it is based on scientific evidence) can be overthrown with new, contrary data. Thus, science, like democracy, has within it the mechanism for renewal and progress, building on earlier knowledge to achieve even better results.

I have included quotations from the legislation to illustrate the detail and vigor with which the scientific method is advocated in the legislation, and that the method is one that real scientists would recognize and adhere to (with the usual quibbling that scientists are prone to). The quotations also illustrate the gamut of educational programs and practices that are now privy to constraints involving scientific evidence of effectiveness. The imperfections in the legislation are also apparent, but these consist mostly of issues of implementation rather than principle, in my view. The centrality of research for actual practice in schools, and, thus, of institutions that generate research, such as colleges and universities (but also foundations, federal agencies and other institutions) is plain. The urgent need for new and better training for educators and leaders (especially deans of colleges of education) is evident, but is presently virtually unmet.

Although researchers should feel encouraged that what they do is so strongly valued, there will no doubt be a tendency to defend past research, disciplinary turf, or the way things used to be. I should point out that there have been successes in the past. Administrators of the National Institute of Education, a previous incarnation of the Institute of Education Sciences, advocated some similar policies and created such noteworthy programs as "scholars in residence," an excellent idea for attracting successful and highly qualified scientists to government service. With that homage to the past, I would encourage researchers, educators, and policy makers to put aside narrow concerns and turn to the future. What are the assessments that ensure accountability, but also inform teachers about areas of learning that need attention, and place the lowest possible burden on the valuable instructional time of students? How do we foster content knowledge as well as reasoning or critical thinking, both essential in the modern economy? What kind of research education is necessary for practitioners to achieve conceptual understanding of learning so that they can successfully adapt effective practices to different contexts and populations? These are only some of the questions that could be asked, but they illustrate the lack of sound scientific answers about basic issues in education. Many researchers continue to urge the use of exploratory methods for hypothesis generation in education after decades of like research. I would submit that there is a surfeit of hypotheses, intuitive speculations, and plausible claims, and a corresponding scarcity of supportive empirical evidence. The most practical achievement of research at this time would be the development of empirically tested theories of learning that could be used to reliably predict which instructional practices will produce which outcomes for which students. Few agencies or foundations are supporting this kind of explanatory and predictive research. The *No Child Left Behind Act* and the *Education Sciences Reform Act* provide opportunities to harness the power of science, including predictive theory, to allow every student access to the American dream. Drawing from multiple disciplines, a new kind of researcher will be needed to achieve this goal, the *educational scientist*.

REFERENCES

American Psychological Association. (2002). Making a difference to education: Will psychology pass up the chance? *APA Monitor, 33,* 76-78.

American Psychological Society. (2003). Science goes to school. APS *Observer, 16*(4), http://www.psycholigical science.org/observer/getArticle.cfm?id=1245

Ashcraft, M. H., & Kirk, E. P. (2001). The relationship among working memory, math anxiety, and performance. *Journal of Experimental Psychology—General, 130,* 224–237.

Bjorklund, D. F. (1995). *Children's thinking: Developmental function and individual differences* (2nd ed.). Pacific Grove, CA: Brooks/Cole.

Campbell, D.T . & Stanley, J. C. (1963). *Experimental and quasi-experimental designs for research.* Boston: Houghton Mifflin.

Carpenter, T. P., Fennema, E., Peterson, P. L., Chiang, C., & Loef. (1989). Using knowledge of children's mathematics thinking in classroom teaching: An experimental study. *American Educational Research Journal, 26,* 499–531.

Cronbach, L. (1982). *Designing evaluations of educational and social programs.* San Francisco, CA: Jossey-Bass.

The Elementary and Secondary Education Act as Reauthorized by the *No Child Left Behind Act of 2001*; Public Law 107-110, Passed January 8, 2002.

Education Sciences Reform Act, Public Law 107-279, Passed November 5, 2002.

Halpern, D. F. (2003). *Thought and knowledge: An introduction to critical thinking* (4th ed.). Mahwah, NJ: Lawrence Erlbaum Associates.

Levin, J. R., & O'Donnell, A. M. (1999). What to do about educational research's credibility gaps? *Issues in Education: Contributions from Educational Psychology, 5,* 177–229.

Mosteller, F., & Boruch, R. (2002). *Evidence matters: Randomized trials in education research.* Washington, DC: Brookings Institution Press.

Nisbett, R., & Ross. L. (1980). *Human inference: Strategies and shortcomings of social judgment.* New York: Academic Press.

Nye, B., Hedges, L. V., & Konstantopoulos, S. (2001). The long-term effects of small classes in early grades: Lasting benefits in mathematics achievement at grade 9. *Journal of Experimental Education, 69,* 245–257.

Reyna, V. F. (in press). Why scientific research? The importance of evidence in changing educational practice. In P. McCardle & V. Chhabra (Eds.), *The voice of evidence: Bringing research to classroom educators.*

Reyna, V. F., Brainerd, C. J., Effken, J., Bootzin, R., & Lloyd, F. J. (2001). The psychology of human computer mismatches. In C. Wolfe (Ed.) *Learning and teaching on the World Wide Web* (pp. 23-44). San Diego, CA: Academic Press.

Schwartz, B., & Reisberg, D. (1991). *Learning and memory.* New York: W.W. Norton.

Shavelson, R. J., & Towne, L. (Eds.). (2002). *Scientific research in education.* Washington, DC: National Academy Press.

Siegler, R. S. (1988). Strategy choices, procedures, and the development of multi-
plication skill. *Journal of Experimental Psychology: General, 117,* 258–275.
Siegler, R. S. (1991). *Children's thinking* (2nd ed.). Englewood Cliffs, NJ: Prentice-
Hall.
Slavin, R. E. (in press). Evidence-based education policies: Transforming educa-
tional practice and research. *Educational Leadership.*

CHAPTER 2

A MATTER OF PROOF

Why Achievement ≠ Learning

Patricia A. Alexander and Michelle M. Riconscente

In her article, "The *No Child Left Behind Act* [NCLB] and scientific research," Valerie Reyna sets forth strong and impassioned arguments for the merits of the *NCLB* (The Elementary and Secondary Education Act, PL 107-110, 2002) and related legislative and programmatic offshoots. Those arguments are framed around scientific evidence drawn from theory and research in cognition and cognitive science. Rather than deal broadly with the elements or implications of *NCLB*, our intention is to examine Dr. Reyna's claims that *NCLB* and related legislation and programs will contribute to better learning for all students. In arguing our position, we, like Dr. Reyna, will draw on the research in cognition, including the extensive literatures in expertise, assessment, individual differences, and motivation, highlighting concerns that potentially challenge the logic of *NCLB* mandates.

Throughout Dr. Reyna's article and the *NCLB* law itself, as well as in much of the surrounding discussion, there is the tendency to equate "achievement" with "learning" by casting achievement as an exhaustive

The No Child Left Behind *Legislation:*
Educational Research and Federal Funding, 27–36
Copyright © 2005 by Information Age Publishing
All rights of reproduction in any form reserved.

representation of the outcome of learning. However, it is our premise that the current conceptual and operational definitions of achievement conflict with the research on learning in critical ways—ways that ultimately negate the claims that *NCLB* will result in better learning for all students. In support of our premise, we will forward seven axioms grounded in decades of research.

LEARNING IS MUCH BROADER THAN ACHIEVEMENT OF BASIC SKILLS IN THRESHOLD DOMAINS

In her discussion of the federal perspective on scientific evidence, Reyna (this issue, p. 7) underscores that a "theme that permeates" *NCLB* and the *Education Sciences Reform Act* is the "need for greater emphasis on *learning...*" While it may seem justified to use the term learning to capture the initiatives exemplified by *NCLB* and other educational programs, there are critical conceptual differences between learning and the nature of achievement targeted in those undertakings. For one, the term "achievement," as annexed by educational policy, has come to signify performance on high-stakes tests, especially those intended to document progress in threshold domains like reading and mathematics. Thus, when we read about efforts to "raise student achievement" (Reyna, this issue, p. 12), we understand that the agenda is test performance and not the broader and more elusive concept of learning. Moreover, the learning required to perform (i.e., achieve) at such a basic level stands in sharp contrast to the conceptualization of learning associated with continued growth and development in content domains.

Specifically, from the extensive literature on expertise and academic development, we know that any comprehensive description of learning must embrace its highly complex and multidimensional nature, and involve extensive representations of students' content knowledge and strategic processing (Bransford, Brown, & Cocking, 2000; Olson & Biolsi, 1991). Further, research findings challenge the assumption that learning happens in discrete steps, such that basic skills must be mastered before students receive instruction in higher-order thinking skills (Glaser, 1986; Resnick, 1987; Zohar & Dori, 2003). Moreover, scientifically-based research is increasingly revealing the impact of affective and conative factors on learning processes and outcomes, and demonstrating that those factors are themselves shaped by the learning process (Dweck & Leggett, 1988; Graham & Weiner, 1996; Murphy & Alexander, 2002; Zimmerman, 2000). In short, the learning associated with achievement of basic skills cannot be conceptually equated to what we know about learning broadly—especially the learning requisite to attaining competence in complex domains of thinking and performance.

At this point, a reader of this commentary might want to dismiss our stated concern as trivial, a matter of semantics. Were the problems of equating achievement (à la *NCLB*) and learning merely definitional ones, then we could settle for semantic fine-tuning. However, we see such definitional latitude as symptomatic of more deeply rooted misconceptions underlying current assessment practices and curricular mandates.

THE TESTING OF BASIC KNOWLEDGE OR SKILLS DOES NOT EQUAL THE ASSESSMENT OF ACADEMIC LEARNING

We accept the premise that the educational system cannot function without assessment, where assessment represents the "process of obtaining information that is used to make educational decisions about students, to give feedback to the student about his or her progress, strengths, weaknesses, to judge instructional effectiveness and curricular adequacy, and to inform policy" (American Federation of Teachers, National Council of Measurement in Education, & National Educational Association, 1990). The point is that assessment does not mean tests. That is, we know that tests, even reliable and valid tests, are but one dimension of assessment and, at their best, afford merely a sampling of human knowledge and abilities. Therefore, to treat test performance as the sole marker of student achievement—to say nothing of student learning—is to speculate unwisely beyond the data.

Moreover, we know that students' processing abilities, content knowledge, affect, and beliefs can be assessed in various ways that yield differing kinds of information, useful for some purposes and not for others (Mislevy, 1994). The more an assessment's methods, feedback, timeframes are tailored to its explicit purposes, the more the conclusions and advice it delivers will be useful and accurate (Pellegrino, Chudowsky, & Glaser, 2001). Consequently, large-scale assessments designed to measure students' broad content knowledge are generally inappropriate diagnostic and instructional tools, because they cannot provide feedback geared to available instructional options and are administered without knowledge of individual students and the academic contexts in which they have been engaged (Braun & Mislevy, 2004). Instruction is best served by formative feedback on student progress situated in a specific context and, thus, requires that characteristics of students be taken into consideration to make the most valid inferences (Baxter, Elder, & Glaser, 1996; Mislevy, 1994).

TEACHING FOR LEARNING SHOULD CONSIST OF MORE THAN TEACHING FOR ACHIEVEMENT

Having introduced the distinction between achievement and learning, we briefly present empirical research that suggests that when test performance is imposed as the ultimate goal of instruction, students learn less than those instructed in conditions in which learning is explicitly made the aim. Using an experimental design, Deci, Spiegel, Ryan, Koestner, and Kauffman (1982) found that teachers who were instructed to facilitate learning employed more strategies associated with higher academic attainment than those told to focus on getting students up to standards. These findings were replicated and extended by Flink, Boggiano, and Barrett (1990), who found that teachers told to ensure that students perform well engaged in controlling instructional strategies, resulting in lower student performance than students whose teachers were told to facilitate learning. In light of these and other findings (e.g., Grolnick & Ryan, 1987; Ryan & Connell, 1989), the flaws in advocating "teaching to a … test" (Reyna, this issue, p. 6) begin to become apparent.

ACQUIRING CONTENT KNOWLEDGE AND HIGHER-ORDER SKILLS ARE SIMULTANEOUS PROCESSES

The research literature reveals much about the processes by which students develop content knowledge, as well as higher-order thinking skills such as problem solving and transfer (Frederiksen, 1984; Lesgold, 1988; Schwartz & Bransford, 1998; Singley & Anderson, 1989). Higher-order thinking skills are generally acknowledged as crucial to individuals' ability to function and contribute in today's society. While it may be intuitive to proceed as if students first learn basic skills and are only then prepared to move on to the demands of higher-order thinking, research demonstrates that, on the contrary, students acquire *both* basic and higher-order thinking more effectively when the latter is integrated into instruction from the outset.

For example, Zohar and Dori (2003) found that students with low prior academic achievement demonstrated substantial gains in content and reasoning processes when engaged in tasks involving higher-order thinking skills. This approach to instruction is not new and has been suggested and explored in reading and mathematics, as well as in other domains (Greeno, 1991; Pellegrino et al., 2001).

NO MANNER OF INSTRUCTION OR ASSESSMENT CAN ELIMINATE INDIVIDUAL DIFFERENCES

One of the more troublesome aspects of current educational rhetoric and policies is the mistaken notion that effective instruction or a systemic program of assessment in any form will result in equity of abilities and performance. The very name of the legislation, "No Child Left Behind," is a proclamation of such misguided assumptions. As Reyna (this issue, p. 7) wrote: "The assumption is that children will be emotionally healthier if they are successful academically, *all other factors being equal*" (our emphasis). The problem is that it is well established that all things are never equal when it comes to human learning and development. Human variability cannot be legislated away.

Certainly, every student deserves the opportunity to succeed to the best of his or her abilities, and it is unjust to assume that academic triumphs or tribulations should be experienced disproportionately and routinely by any racial, ethnic, gender, or socioeconomic group. Yet, to assume that we could find a way to ensure that "all students will read at grade level" is to make hollow claims with no bases in scientific evidence. After all, "at grade level" is but an academic expectation built on knowledge of *typical* performance defined by mathematical *averages* (Lyman, 1991; McMillan, 1997). Implicit in the use of an average is that some students will be above and some students below this typical performance. If it were conceivable that "at grade level" could be realized for all students, it would be necessary to reassess what this very concept means. We would have to move the bar higher so that such a standard remained a true marker of typical performance, rather than the starting point for learning and assessment (Popham, 1995).

Even more to the point, there is reason to assume that effective instruction suited to the broad conceptualization of learning forwarded herein would potentially exacerbate human differences, rather than eliminate them (Stanovich, 1986). Simply stated, those who have not only the fundamental skills in threshold domains, but also have the ability to think critically and problem solve effectively; a base of principled knowledge relative to an academic topic or domain; and, the interest, goals, and desire to pursue understanding will continue to make strides toward competency and expertise (Alexander, Jetton, & Kulikowich, 1995; Ericsson & Smith, 1993). Those who are limited in any one of these dimensions face the risk of being left behind in their academic journeys (Alexander, 2003). Learning environments or curricula that promote one or more of these dimensions of academic development will not be experienced equally by students as a consequence of their existing state of knowledge, strategic ability, or motivations (Hidi, 1990; Kardash, Royer, & Greene, 1988).

Thus, individual differences that pre-exist any educational experiences ensure that variability in learning will result from those experiences.

Theoretically, the only way to achieve the end of all students at grade level would be to institute ineffective and biased instruction that would guarantee that students who already possess certain cognitive and motivational advantages are not permitted to draw on those resources. These students would be academically confined or constrained for as long as it would take for others to catch up. Of course, the developmental ramifications of such an action are almost inconceivable and the loss of human potential devastating.

IT IS THE STUDENT, NOT THE CLASSROOM OR SCHOOL, THAT LEARNS WELL OR POORLY

In turning to implications for research and practice, we draw attention to an additional issue that surfaces in Reyna's comments and the *NCLB* legislation. Simply stated, the unit of analysis on which programmatic, accountability, and instructional decisions are to be based has little to do with individual student learning and development. This observation stands in sharp contrast to the decades of research on learning centered on the individual (Ackerman, 2003; Gustafsson, & Undheim, 1996). For example, Reyna (this issue, p. 6) writes that "*schools that excel* well beyond minimum standards do not have to be concerned about assessments of basic skills; such *advanced students* should easily pass basic-skills tests" (our emphases). Later she refers to high achieving and low-performing schools. However, it is the students, not schools, that learn and individual students who either meet or fail to meet educational expectations.

Here there is a clear confounding of measures of overall school achievement with that of individual students. To highlight this tendency in *NCLB*, we point out that in the legislation the word "school" is used nearly 4,000 times (over 10 times more than "individual") and appears over twice as frequently as "student." It is appealing to think of curricular modifications to address serious student needs in terms of a triage model, for instance, as suggested by Reyna. However, when assessments and curricula remain focused on the collective in the form of an educational institution, triage becomes tantamount to administering invasive emergency treatments to entire populations, including those who demonstrate no symptoms or even show evidence of being academically healthy.

What is not clear in the legislation, or in Reyna's comments, is the intended scope of *NCLB*-mandated curricular changes. Are mandated curricular changes necessarily schoolwide? If so, are provisions in place for schoolwide programs and curricula responsive to the needs of individual students? Insights gleaned from decades of research persuasively indicate that expectations for success in a one-size-fits-all paradigm are unfounded (Byrnes, 2001; Ku & Sullivan, 2002).

SCIENTIFIC EVIDENCE IS CONDITIONAL EVIDENCE

As educational researchers, we acquire the wise habit of qualifying our findings. We speak about what is significant, for whom, and under what conditions. The community of practice looks down upon attempts to generalize beyond the data. That may not make for exciting press or salacious sound bites, but it is the nature of evidence in social science. Thus, when we read about the evidence presented in support of some initiative, program, or technique, we expect the necessary conditions to be clearly explicated. When initiatives, programs, or techniques, even well studied programs like *Reading First* or *Success for All*, are presented without qualifications, we become the intelligent skeptics that Reyna described. We want to know what the potential educational shortcomings or side effects for an intervention might be. We want to know what will become of those few or those many who are not the specific targets of such interventions, but who come to feel the effects either through direct exposure or by secondary means.

In essence, we do not expect to hear simply about "educational programs and practices that have been clearly demonstrated to be effective through scientific research" (Reyna, this issue, p. 7). We expect to read about the specific outcomes supported by the data, the characteristics of those who benefit, as well as the characteristics of those who do not. We also want to know what is to become of those who begin to show the positive effects of some particular intervention. When does the "treatment" stop? When is a program of educational wellness to be instituted in lieu of a program of educational deficiencies?

CONCLUSION

As educational psychologists, we are the first to defend and promote the advancement of rigorous scientific methods in conducting educational research, and the importance of its application to educational practice. However, the entire push for scientifically-based research crumbles with the equating of achievement to learning. Research has yielded countless insights and directions for further investigation for the improvement of learning. Despite such insights, the *NCLB* legislation tethers instruction, curricula, educational research, and accountability to "increases in student achievement," and in so doing threatens to impoverish the very process it sought to rescue. Again we return to the fundamental issue of how achievement is defined. Equating learning to achievement as measured on large-scale assessments, and then mandating increased achievement according to this conception, undermines the goal of education, and the good intentions that undoubtedly are at the origin of the *NCLB* legislation itself. Rather than leave no child behind, let us harness our knowledge and resources to support all children in their journeys toward academic competence.

REFERENCES

Ackerman, P. L. (2003). Cognitive ability and non-ability trait determinants of expertise. *Educational Researcher, 32,* 15–20.

Alexander, P. A. (2003). The development of expertise: The journey from acclimation to proficiency. *Educational Researcher, 32,* 10–14.

Alexander, P. A., Jetton, T. L., & Kulikowich, J. M. (1995). Interrelationship of knowledge, interest, and recall: Assessing a model of domain learning. *Journal of Educational Psychology, 87,* 559–575.

American Federation of Teachers, National Council of Measurement in Education, & National Educational Association. (1990). *Standards for teacher competence in educational assessment of students.* Washington, DC: American Psychological Association.

Baxter, G. P., Elder, A. D., & Glaser, R. (1996). Knowledge-based cognition and performance assessment in the science classroom. *Educational Psychologist, 31,* 133–140.

Bransford, J. D., Brown, A. L., & Cocking, R. R. (2000). *How people learn: Brain, mind, experience, and school.* Washington, DC: National Academy Press.

Braun, H. I., & Mislevy, R. J. (2004). *Intuitive test theory.* CSE Technical Report. Los Angeles: The National Center for Research on Evaluation, Standards, Student Testing (CRESST), Center for Studies in Education, UCLA.

Byrnes, J. P. (2001). *Cognitive development and learning in instructional contexts.* Boston: Allyn & Bacon.

Deci. E. L., Spiegel, N. H., Ryan, R. M., Koestner, R., & Kauffman, M. (1982). *Journal of Educational Psychology, 74,* 852–859.

Dweck, C. S., & Leggett, E. L. (1988). A social-cognitive approach to motivation and personality. *Psychological Review, 95,* 256–272.

The Elementary and Secondary Education Act as Reauthorized by the *No Child Left Behind Act of 2001*; Public Law 107-110, Passed January 8, 2002.

Ericsson, K. A., & Smith, J. (1993). *Toward a general theory of expertise: Prospects and limits.* New York: Cambridge University Press.

Flink, C. Boggiano, A. K., & Barrett, M. (1990). Controlling teacher strategies: Undermining children's self-determination and performance. *Journal of Personality and Social Psychology, 59,* 916–924.

Frederiksen, N. (1984). Implication of cognitive theory for instruction in problem solving. *Review of Educational Research, 54*, 363–407.

Glaser, R. (1986). Education and thinking: The role of knowledge. *American Psychologist, 39*, 93–104.

Graham, S., & Weiner, B. (1996). Theories and principles of motivation. In D. C. Berliner & R. C. Calfee (Eds.), *Handbook of educational psychology* (pp. 63–84). New York: Macmillan.

Greeno, J. G. (1991). Number sense as situated knowing in a conceptual domain. *Journal for Research in Mathematics Education, 22*, 170–218.

Grolnick, W. S., & Ryan, R. M. (1987). Autonomy in children's learning: An experimental and individual difference investigation. *Journal of Personality and Social Psychology, 52*, 890–898.

Gustafsson, J.-E., & Undheim, J. O. (1996). Individual differences in cognitive functions. In D. C. Berliner & R. C. Calfee (Eds.), *Handbook of educational psychology* (pp. 186–242). New York: Macmillan.

Hidi, S. (1990). Interest and its contribution as a mental resource for learning. *Review of Educational Research, 60*, 549–571.

Kardash, C. A., Royer, J. M., & Greene, B. A. (1988). Effects of schemata on both encoding and retrieval of information from prose. *Journal of Educational Psychology, 80*, 324–329.

Ku, H. Y., & Sullivan, H. J. (2002). Student performance and attitudes using personalized mathematics instruction. *Educational Technology Research and Development, 50*, 21–34.

Lesgold, A. M. (1988). Problem solving. In R. J. Sternberg & E. E. Smith (Eds.), *The psychology of human thoughts* (pp. 188–213). New York: Cambridge University Press.

Lyman, H. B. (1991). *Test scores and what they mean.* Englewood Cliffs, NJ: Prentice Hall.

McMillan, J. H. (1997). *Classroom assessment: Principles and practice for effective instruction.* Boston: Allyn & Bacon.

Mislevy, R. M. (1994). Evidence and inference in educational assessment. *Psychometrika, 59*, 439–483.

Murphy, P. K., & Alexander, P. A. (2002). What counts? The predictive powers of subject-matter knowledge, strategic processing, and interest in domain-specific performance. *Journal of Experimental Education, 70*, 197–214.

Olson, J. R., & Biolsi, K. J. (1991). Techniques for representing expert knowledge. In K. A. Ericsson & J. Smith (Eds.), *Toward a general theory of expertise: Prospects and limits* (pp. 240–285). New York: Cambridge University Press.

Pellegrino, J. W., Chudowsky, N., & Glaser, R. (2001). *Knowing what students know: The science and design of educational assessment.* Washington, DC: National Academy Press.

Popham, W. J. (1995). *Classroom assessment: What teachers need to know.* Boston: Allyn & Bacon.

Resnick, L. B. (1987). *Education and learning to think.* Washington, DC: National Academy Press.

Reyna, V. (2005). The *No Child Left Behind Act* and scientific research: A view from Washington, DC. In J. S. Carlson & J. R. Levin (Eds.), *Scientifically-based educa-*

tion research and federal funding agencies: The case of the No Child Left Behind *legislation* (Vol. 1, pp. 1-25). Greenwich, CT: Information Age.

Ryan, R. M., & Connell, J. P. (1989). Perceived locus of causality and internalization: Examining reasons for acting in two domains. *Journal of Personality and Social Psychology, 57,* 749–761.

Schwartz, D. L., & Bransford, J. D. (1998). A time for telling. *Cognition and Instruction, 16,* 475–522.

Singley, K., & Anderson, J. R. (1989). *The transfer of cognitive skill.* Cambridge, MA: Harvard University Press.

Stanovich, K. E. (1986). Matthew effects in reading: Some consequences of individual differences in the acquisition of literacy. *Reading Research Quarterly, 21,* 360–407.

Zimmerman, B. J. (2000). Self-efficacy: An essential motive to learn. *Contemporary Educational Psychology, 25,* 82–91.

Zohar, A., & Dori, Y. (2003). Higher order thinking skills and low-achieving students: Are they mutually exclusive? *Journal of the Learning Sciences, 12,* 145–181.

CHAPTER 3

FEDERAL INTRUSION IN RESEARCH AND TEACHING AND THE MEDICAL MODEL MYTH

Richard L. Allington

There are days when I'm moved to gather together a few friends from the dismal education research community and work with them to develop guidelines for medical research and education (and the necessary qualifications for medical deans). Any number of powerful pundits and policy makers have asserted that education should be more like the medical profession. I've already laid bare much of the fallacy of such arguments (Allington, 2002), as have others (e.g., Cunningham, 2001; 2003), but Dr. Reyna has moved me to revisit this issue.

RANDOMIZED TRIALS AS EVIDENCE?

Consider the following unscientific assertions (from Cunningham, 2003):

The No Child Left Behind *Legislation:*
Educational Research and Federal Funding, 37–47
Copyright © 2005 by Information Age Publishing
All rights of reproduction in any form reserved.

- Obesity increases the risk of heart disease.
- Women who are pregnant should not drink alcohol.
- Cigarette smoking increases the likelihood of lung cancer.

The assertions are unscientific because there have been no randomized experiments testing their accuracy. No one has randomly assigned children or adults to groups who were purposely forced to eat far more calories than they expended. Nor has any scientist randomly assigned some women to drink alcohol during pregnancy while ensuring others do not. Nor has anyone been assigned to a smoking group. In fact there exist few randomized studies portraying healthy people exhibiting normal development. Instead, studies of the efficacy of pharmaceutical products, for instance, are typically tested against a narrow population of subjects for whom the treatment may be beneficial. Rather than a random selection from the whole population, a randomized selective sample is used. Epidemiological studies, the sort that provide the evidence for the assertions above, examine larger normal populations (e.g., nurses) and draw correlations between certain lifestyle features and the incidence of various health issues. But correlation is not causation as we are often reminded. Nonetheless, federal health agencies, medical associations, and others use such correlational data to create guidelines for human behaviors. Given what we have learned in such studies about the risk of some lifestyle features it is typically considered unethical to run randomized experiments. So much for truly randomized medical experiments to find the truth.

EVIDENCE-BASED PRACTICE?

Further, contrary to Dr. Reyna's assertion that "it is unimaginable to administer untested drugs to patients," just such practice is commonplace in medicine, especially in pediatrics. As Mark Isaac, director of a pediatric foundation, has noted (Kaufman & Connolly, 2002), "Seventy-five percent of drugs used in America have never been tested for use by children at all." Every single day doctors in this country prescribe "unscientific" drugs for patients of all sorts. In fact, according medical researchers, something like 80% of all medical decisions are based on personal experience, tradition, and intuition, not on scientific evidence (Hitt, 2001).

Perhaps that is because "Physicians have been trained in such a manner that they have no idea how to read from the original medical literature or how to interpret it" according internal medicine specialist Gordon H. Guyatt, co-author of a paper on this topic in the *Journal of the American Medical Association* (Patterson & Guyatt, 2002). There is little evidence that medical practice is or ever has been evidence-based if we are imagining physicians reading about the latest scientific results in medical research journals and then using those findings in daily practice. Most physicians do not seem even to follow the summary guidelines for treatments developed from the scientific research. A recent report in the *New England Journal of Medicine*, for instance, found that:

> Doctors fail to take nearly half the recommended steps for treating common illnesses such as high blood pressure and diabetes, suggesting health care in the United States isn't nearly as good as many people thought. (Associated Press, 2003, p. A1)

Finally, in a case of the pot calling the kettle black, while supporting high-stakes testing, Reyna provides no scientific evidence that the imposition of such mandates on schools will improve student achievement. There seems to be no such evidence (Strauss, 2002). So while mandating evidence-based practice in schools, federal policy makers impose the enormously expensive but untested fad of high-stakes testing on children. And then the federal bureaucrats and their advisors rant on and on about faddism in schools!

We do have testimony as to the effects of similar accountability practices in medicine however. According to Jauhar (2001), the federal mandate that hospitals report mortality outcomes of cardiac surgery has placed enormous pressures on doctors to produce "good" outcomes—that is to report fewer deaths, But this seems to have restricted access to such surgery by higher-risk patients. As one physician reported, "Hospitals are gaming the system. Those getting cited are now turning down high-risk patients. Some of the so-called best hospitals are only doing the most straightforward cases."

This scenario sounds strikingly similar to the reports from Birmingham (AL) of hundreds of low-achieving high-school students being "dropped" from the rolls just before statewide testing began (Orel, 2003) or the thousands of students in the Houston (TX) schools who simply vanished from the accountability scheme (Archer, 2003) during the "Texas Miracle." High-stakes testing initiatives have been statistically linked to increased flunking and special education placements, neither of which is a "scientific" solution to the problem of low achievement (Allington & McGill-Franzen, 1992). Flunking is another one of those currently popular political mandates for which not a shred of evidence of efficacy is available. And mandated flunking has been implemented in a number of states and large cities, all without a whisper of concern from those federal policy makers who pretend to be interested in evidence-based educational practice.

IDEOLOGY VERSUS EVIDENCE

In some imaginary place there may be such a thing as pure science along with pure procedures for interpreting that science and communicating the findings in a reliable and unbiased way. But neither medicine nor education seems to be located in the same universe as the imaginary place. Even the *Wall Street Journal* lamented the triumph of ideology over expertise in the current administration's appointment of the "scientific" panel to review the research on safety standards for lead in children's blood (Begley, 2002). The same has been said about the National Reading Panel and other recent education advisory panels (e.g, Garan, 2001; Krashen, 2001; Metcalf, 2002; Pressley, 2002).

As Scarr (1985) noted, "We do not discover scientific facts, we invent them." The belief that only experimental research is "scientific" is an invention, not a fact. Consider that we have no "scientific" evidence on children's language acquisition, if only because no one could ethically randomly assign newborns to debilitating language environments. Similarly, we don't have good "scientific" evidence on an issue such as the value of promoting wide, independent reading among children. No one would randomly assign children to a "no reading until age 10" control group.

But, as with the evidence on obesity, smoking, and language acquisition, the lack of randomized trials research is hardly a reason for the federally-funded and widely distributed Put Reading First (PRF) (Armbruster, Lehr & Osborn, 2001) guide to research-based reading instruction to inform teachers that "Rather than allocating instructional time for independent reading, encourage your children to read more out of school." There is an overwhelming body of evidence on the critical role of the volume of reading to reading development (Allington, 2001; Stanovich, 2000). There are good reasons that research has few randomized experiments. But working with patterns of natural variation in cross-sectional and correlational studies, the issue of volume is repeatedly demonstrated to be important. Asserting a lack of evidence for independent reading practice parallels the tobacco lobby's primary legal defense of cigarette companies (Cunningham, 2001)

Likewise, when PRF asserts that "Systematic and explicit phonics instruction is particularly beneficial for children who are having difficulty learning to read … and in helping children overcome reading difficulties," it is a misrepresentation of the NRP finding that, "Phonics instruction failed to exert a significant impact on the reading performance of low-achieving readers in 2nd through 6th grade." When PRF states that "Adding phonics workbooks or phonics worksheets to these [basal and literature-based] programs of instruction has not been effective. Such add-ons confuse rather than help children to read," one wonders. As Tim Shanahan (2003), NRP panel member recently wrote, "NRP did not find that and, given the nature of the research findings we reported on phonics, I would be surprised if the statement were true." It seems that ideology trumps evidence in Washington.

CONTINGENT EVIDENCE AND PROFESSIONAL WISDOM (INTUITION) IN MEDICINE AND EDUCATION

A central problem for both medical and educational researchers is the contingent nature of all "facts," reported from research studies, even those from randomized trials. In an editorial in the *New England Journal of Medicine*, Edward Frohlich discusses two large-scale, longitudinal studies of ACE inhibitors and diuretics on the incidence of "cardiovascular events in elderly hypertensive patients." The two studies came to different conclusions. He discusses what physicians might make of the conflicting findings given that the two studies differed in several ways.

Frohlich notes a basic problem with such intervention studies is that they are at best a proxy for the care provided by individual patients by their own physicians. For instance,

Patients with hypertension—particularly elderly patients—frequently have associated coexisting conditions. If a patient has diabetes, it would certainly be wise to initiate therapy with an ACE inhibitor.... If a patient has cardiac failure, one might use both a diuretic and an ACE inhibitor.... If there is a history of myocardial infarction, an ACE inhibitor diminishes the risks of future cardiac failure ... a beta-blocker is also indicated for such a patient.... If the patient has angina pectoris ... it may be wise to use a calcium antagonist ... to prevent strokes.... In selecting appropriate therapy, choose a drug or a combination of drugs for which there is strong evidence of effectiveness in persons with the type of problem found in the patient.... In choosing between a diuretic and an ACE inhibitor, the physician can make a reasonable selection by reviewing the patient's history and course.... We must remember that trials describe population averages for the purposes of developing guidelines, whereas physicians must focus on the individual patient's clinical responses.

He concludes that:

Whereas epidemiologists focus on responses at the population level in order to develop therapeutic guidelines, health care providers must deal with the specific relationship between the physician and the patient. This relationship is where the therapeutic tire meets the road, and there is no place for absolute or categorical answers. Population-based studies of therapies help point the way but are not analogous to the care of individual patients.

In other words, the "scientific" treatment of patients depends on the patient and the particular characteristics the patient displays. Not all patients respond positively to the same treatment. Patients, like children, vary in their individual characteristics. In a similar vein, Torgeson (2000) notes that in each of five randomized educational intervention experiments there were "treatment resisters." Each study examined the impact of some sort of code-emphasis intervention with elementary-age children experiencing severe reading problems. In all studies there were some children (12–46%) who benefited little from the interventions, even the tutorial interventions. This even though the outcome measures were phonological tasks and word list reading, the focus of the intervention designs. He notes that:

> We found that phonological abilities were clearly important [in estimating success], but they were not more important than socioeconomic background and teachers' ratings of behavior and attention in the classroom.

In other words, treatment effectiveness depended on children's individual characteristics.

Similarly, McNaughton, Phillips, and MacDonald (2003) report that while children from cultural and linguistic minority groups achieved normal levels of proficiency in the phonological and letter knowledge as a result of their reading instruction, markedly lower progress was made on text reading, writing, and word reading. They note, "The implication is that the instructional procedures that are particularly effective for accelerating text reading and writing may not be the same as instruction that is effective solely for developing decoding skills." The reading instruction they observed was, on the other hand, far more effective in developing the text reading and writing of children from the cultural majority.

One reason teachers may pay little attention to the research reports is that they know that good teaching is an "it depends," contingent, situational, task. When the research is filled with studies that measure primarily phonological and decoding skills acquisition and fail to monitor text reading, writing development, and comprehension (as was the case for the majority of studies reviewed by the NRP), the instructional recommendations derived from those studies may have little relevance to the primary goal of classroom teachers—producing children who can read texts with understanding. Many teachers already know, from experience, that unbalanced instruction creates unbalanced readers. They don't need meta-analyses of the research (e.g, Camilli,Vargas, & Yurecko, 2003; Swanson, Trainin, Necoechea, & Hammil, 2003) to know that code-emphasis instruction and a focus on phonological skills development have little impact on children's text reading and comprehension, regardless of the ideological stance in Washington. And teachers know children differ in their responsiveness to different instructional foci and routines. Gradually, the research community may discover what teachers already know as a fact— children differ.

For a half-century, federal education bureaucrats, with the support of naïve members of Congress, have pushed top-down initiatives as the "proven" method to stimulate improved achievement. If federal policy makers were the least bit interested in what the research says they might examine the effectiveness of these several initiatives. What they would find is a consistent record of the failure of these initiatives to improve student achievement (Allington & Nowak, 2004). Quoting from the independent evaluations of two of the largest federal top-down initiatives, *Comprehensive School Reform Development* and *Project FollowThrough*:

> The initial hypothesis, that by adopting a whole-school design a school could improve its performance was largely unproved. (Berends, Bodilly, & Kirby, 2002)

> If the concentrated effort of highly competent and well-funded sponsors with a few sites cannot produce uniform results from locality to locality, it seems doubtful that any model program could (House, Glass, McLean, & Walker, 1978).

In other words, for those who haven't looked at the flatness of the trend data on the NAEP since 1970, all these federal "proven" programs seem to work in some places but never produce the sort of broad success that policy makers imagined or entrepreneurs hyped. The problem with federal initiatives is (a) they are typically based on historical evidence of what seemed to work in a few sites in the previous decades from their reading of the historical research; (b) they are invariably tainted with ideological fervor that ignores the very findings of the studies they funded; and (c) the root cause is never found to be bad federal designs but teacher resistance to scientific "facts." But, as the cartoon character Dilbert notes, "The definition of insanity is: Doing the same thing over and over and expecting different results."

Too many "scientific" researchers echo Reyna with pronouncements from on high of "what works" and some of those researchers guide policy makers when they create the sort of unworkable mandates that sorely restrict teacher autonomy and, ultimately, undermine any professional (or personal) accountability a teacher might feel. No one feels accountable, nor should they, when they simply 'follow orders" and comply with federal and state mandates about how to teach.

I wish Reyna's ambitious schemes were better informed about the complexities of translating "add-on, pull-out, delivered by experts from afar" instructional research into the daily routines of exemplary teaching (Allington & Johnston, 2002; Pressley et al., 2001; Taylor, Pearson, Peterson & Rodriguez, 2003). I wish she better understood that, as with medical research, treatments in experiments are but a proxy for the actual teacher-student instructional interactions. I wish each of those psychology professors whose research she seems to admire would spend a several hundred days observing in elementary school classrooms, documenting the complexities of good teaching, especially in this era of unscientific federal demands. I wish most of the research that has been used to justify these mandates were routinely examined by a panel of education experts—teachers.

I find the arrogance of federal policy makers and their advisors incredibly unfounded. Good research may help us craft better schools and develop lessons that produce better readers. Good research may help us develop physicians that know better how to help patients avoid or stem obesity or quit smoking cigarettes. But in the end researchers and policy makers may have to realize that in both professions the most effective practitioners rely more on intuition (or professional wisdom developed though experience) than on the evidence produced by "scientists" far from the field and realities of teaching or doctoring.

CONCLUSION

In my view the whole point to the creation of the NRP was to attempt to deliver, under the guise of scientific evidence, on the administration's campaign plank to bring phonics instruction back to schools. The other major education planks—school prayer and vouchers—would be more difficult to deliver compared to finding a small group of like-minded researchers to conclude that systematic phonics was the solution to lackluster improvements in American children's reading achievement. Notice how few of the NRP panelists have objected to the blatant misrepresentations of their findings by at least three different federal agencies (Allington, 2002; Coles, 2003; Cunningham, 2001; Garan, 2001; Krashen, 2001). Notice how few of the policy makers that howl for an end to faddism have offered even a peep of concern on this topic or asked for the evidence on high-stakes testing and flunking.

Consider that had the NRP reviewed the research on motivation and engagement, their findings would conflict with many of the mandates accompanying the federal *Reading First* initiative. Had the NRP examined the reciprocal and beneficial relationship between reading and writing activity, how different classroom reading lessons might look today. Had they examined the experimental research on the role of discussion and conversation about texts that have been read (or written) the whole nature of classroom interactions would be headed, perhaps, in a very different direction. Had they looked at the scientific evidence on the importance of matching children with books where they experience success we might not be watching one-size-fits-all mandates of commercial curriculum materials and whole class lessons dominating in *Reading First* schools.

When research is used selectively to accomplish political and entrepreneurial ends, nothing much good can be expected to result. I really do wish politicians and policy makers gave a hoot about the research on good teaching. But, as I have argued earlier (Allington, 1999), the only data politicians and their policy makers seem much interested in are polling data. The sort of federal intrusion into education, and into classroom instruction and educational research especially, that Reyna celebrates, has little evidence to support it and I doubt that much good will come from it.

REFERENCES

Allington, R. L. (1999). Crafting state educational policy: The slippery role of educational research and researchers. *Journal of Literacy Research, 31*, 457–482.

Allington, R. L. (2001). *What really matters for struggling readers: Designing research-based programs*. Boston: Allyn & Bacon.

Allington, R. L. (2002). *Big brother and the national reading curriculum: How ideology trumped evidence*. Portsmouth, NH: Heinemann.

Allington, R. L., & Johnston, P. H. (Eds.). (2002). *Reading to learn: Lessons from exemplary 4th grade classrooms*. New York: Guilford.

Allington, R. L., & McGill-Franzen, A. (1992). Unintended effects of educational reform in New York State. *Educational Policy, 6*, 396–413.

Allington, R. L., & Nowak, R. (2004). Proven programs and other unscientific ideas. In C. C. Block, D. Lapp, E. J. Cooper, J. Flood, N. Roser, & J. V. Tinajero (Eds.), *Teaching all the children: Strategies for developing literacy in urban settings*. New York: Guilford.

Archer, J. (2003). Houston case offers lesson on dropouts. *Education Week*, pp. 1,14–17.

Armbruster, B., Lehr, F., & Osborn, J. (2001). *Put Reading First: The research building blocks for teaching children to read*. Washington, DC: Partnership for Reading, National Institute for Literacy.

Associated Press. (2003). Study: U.S. physicians neglecting guidelines. *The Gainesville Sun*, p. A1.

Berends, M., Bodilly, S., & Kirby, S. N. (2002). Looking back over a decade of whole-school reform: The experience of New American Schools. *Phi Delta Kappan, 84*, 168–175.

Camilli, G., Vargas, S., & Yurecko, M. (2003). Teaching children to read: The fragile link between science and federal education policy. *Education Policy Analysis Archives, 11*. Retrieved May 20, 2003, from http://epaa.asu.edu/epaa/v11n15/

Coles, G. (2003). *Reading the naked truth: Literacy, legislation, and lies*. Portsmouth, NH: Heinemann.

Cunningham, J. W. (2000). *Learning, remembering, and forgetting to teach reading*. Paper presentation, International Reading Association, Indianapolis, IN.

Cunningham, J. W. (2001). The National Reading Panel report. *Reading Research Quarterly, 30*, 326–335.

Garan, E. (2001). Beyond the smoke and mirrors: A critique of the National Reading Panel Report on phonics. *Phi Delta Kappan, 82*, 500–506.

Hitt, J. (2001, December 9). Evidence-based medicine. *The New York Times Magazine, 22*.

House, E. R., Glass, G. V., McLean, L., & Walker, D. (1978). No simple answers: Critique of the Follow Through evaluations. *Harvard Educational Review, 48*, 128–160.

Jauhar, S. (2001). Life and death stakes in the numbers game. *New York Times*. www.nytimes.com/2001/09/11/health/policy/11essa.html; accessed December 21, 2001.

Kaufman, M., & Connolly, C. (2002, April 20). U.S. backs pediatric tests in reversal on drug safety. *Washington Post*, p. A3.

Krashen, S. (2001). More smoke and mirrors: A critique of the National Reading Panel report on fluency. *Phi Delta Kappan, October*, 119–123.

McNaughton, S., Phillips, G., & MacDonald, S. (2003). Profiling teaching and learning needs in beginning literacy instruction: The case of children in 'low decile' schools in New Zealand. *Journal of Literacy Research, 35*, 703–730.

Metcalf, S. D. (2002, January 28). Reading between the lines. *The Nation*. http://thenation.com.docprint.mhtml?i=20020128&s=metcalf; accessed May 5, 2002.

Orel, S. (2003). Left behind in Birmingham. In G. Pipkin & L. Lent (Eds.), *Silent no more: Voices of courage in American schools* (pp. 1-14). Portsmouth, NH: Heinemann.

Patterson, K. (2002, May 5). What doctors don't know. (Almost everything). *New York Times Magazine*, 74–77.

Pressley, M. (2002). Effective beginning reading instruction. *Journal of Literacy Research, 34*, 165–188.

Pressley, M., Wharton-McDonald, R., Allington, R. L., Block, C. C., Morrow, L., Tracey, D., Baker, K., Brooks, G., Cronin, J., Nelson, E., & Woo, D. (2001). A study of effective first-grade literacy instruction. *Scientific Studies in Reading, 5*, 35–58.

Scarr, S. (1985). Constructing psychology: Making facts and fables for our times. *American Psychologist, 40*, 499–512.

Shanahan, T. (2003). Research-based reading instruction: Myths about the National Reading Panel report. *Reading Teacher, 56*, 646–655.

Stanovich, K. E. (2000). *Progress in understanding reading: Scientific foundations and new frontiers*. New York: Guilford.

Strauss, S. L. (2002). Politics and reading at the National Institute of Child Health and Human Development. *Pediatrics, 109,*143–144.

Swanson, H. L., Trainin, G., Necoechea, D. M., & Hammill, D. D. (2003). Rapid naming, phonological awareness, and reading: A meta-analysis of the correlational evidence. *Review of Educational Research, 73*, 407–440.

Taylor, B. M., Pearson, P. D., Peterson, D. S., & Rodriguez, M. C. (2003). Reading growth in high-poverty classrooms: The influences of teacher practices that encourage cognitive engagement in literacy learning. *Elementary School Journal, 104*, 4–28.

Torgeson, J. K. (2000). Individual differences in response to early interventions in reading: The lingering problem of treatment resisters. *Learning Disabilities Research and Practice, 15*, 55–64.

CHAPTER 4

EDUCATIONAL RESEARCH AND *NCLB*

A View from the Past

Robert C. Calfee

HISTORIES

"Deja vu all over again" is not unusual in political debates, but in the current instance, the events fall within a lifetime—mine. Reyna does not rely much on history other than the image in Figure 1.1, which juxtaposes federal spending and NAEP reading achievement across the past quarter-century or so. The figure, mentioned only in passing, probably intends to illustrate more than prove the point: Despite massive financial infusions from the federal government, student achievement remains "stagnant." In fact, reading has actually improved somewhat in recent decades (cf. Figure 1.2), and mathematics even more, despite significant upturns in the proportion of school children at social and economic risk. And the increased federal investment, which began in the Clinton administration (as did many *NCLB* elements), remains a small proportion of the public school budget.

The No Child Left Behind *Legislation:*
Educational Research and Federal Funding, 49–56
Copyright © 2005 by Information Age Publishing
All rights of reproduction in any form reserved.

Three histories seem to me to merit consideration with regard to *NCLB*. At the federal level, substantial *organizational changes* have occurred during the past few decades: the change in Education from an Office to a Department, the emergence of the National Institute of Education (NIE) modeled on the National Institutes of Health, the establishment of the Center and Laboratory system, the demise of NIE and the birth of the Office of Educational Research and Improvement (OERI), and now the arrival of the Institute for Education Sciences (IES). Each change promised greater research funding and significant impact on educational practice, promises that proved rather hollow. Investments in educational research, including evaluation studies, remain a fraction of 1 percent of the overall cost of the enterprise.

The second history traces prevailing themes in *educational research*. Numerous resources are available in this arena, from the century-long yearbook series of the National Society for the Study of Education to thoughtful monographs (e.g., Lagemann & Shulman, 1999; Cronbach & Suppes, 1969) and most recently the NRC report by Shavelson and Towne (2002, in Reyna). The story recounts the dominance of quantitative methods from Thorndike through the advance of psychometrics during and after the Second World War. The First-Grade Reading Studies (Bond & Dykstra, 1967), perhaps the most notable effort at large-scale field research, demonstrated the difficulty of this approach and the challenges in practical application of findings. It was not a "randomized field experiment," in the sense that no one claimed that students were randomly assigned to treatments. The *Follow Through Study* (Stallings, 1975), also a large-scale field study, made a serious effort to document actual program implementation. In both of these investigations and endeavors, "teachers within program" accounted for a substantial amount of variance in student performance. In the 1970s, NIE actively pursued the incorporation of qualitative methods in its research portfolio, which marked the appearance of remarkable investigations (e.g., Heath's *Ways With Words*, 1983; Cazden's *Classroom Discourse*, 1988; and projects by the Center for the Study of Reading, the Institute for Research on Teaching, and the Center for the Study of Writing) that illuminated mechanisms of teaching and learning. Reyna expresses concern about the decline in quantitative studies in the flagship journals; a review by professional organizations of publication trends might indeed be useful for informing policy.

The third history centers around the *translation of research into practice*. The greatest success here is probably the standardized multiple-choice test, a research artifact that dominates educational policy and practice in remarkable ways. But back to the history, establishment of the federal system of educational centers and laboratories in the 1960s reflected a major effort to connect research and practice. The university centers would do research, and pass it on to the regional laboratories for translation and implementation. The reality proved otherwise. Laboratories built local support for their services, which provided an ongoing basis for continued funding of both labs and centers. Conceptually, the centers were driven to implementation research, and the labs to more basic studies. Centers were to be "mission-oriented," while the labs attended to regions, a design that thwarted collaboration. Along the way, a variety of "What Works" endeavors emerged, including ERIC and the National Dissemination Network.

I am not a historian, but it seems that a study of these previous events might warrant attention. Many generated significant conceptual outcomes, and some influenced practice.

THE TASKS OF EDUCATIONAL RESEARCH

NCLB mandates that, to receive the federal stamp of approval, educational programs must undergo a randomized field trial. It appears that substantial federal dollars will be devoted to such efforts. The methodology is presented as the "gold standard" for other fields, medicine in particular. A "user-friendly" guide is available on the web from the Coalition for Evidence-Based Policy (2003). The basic claim is that randomized assignment of students to experimental treatments assures adequate control for causal claims.

Research, broadly conceived, is about learning and problem solving. Learning is partly a matter of acquiring skill and knowledge, but it also entails curiosity and motivation. Problem solving entails finding and framing the problem; once outside of school, the answers are seldom in the back of the book.

What needs to be "learned" about public schooling, and what problems require significant attention at the national level? Given particular answers to such questions, then what criteria should be established in providing federal funds for "really good research programs?" In my professional lifetime, we have learned a great deal about "school learning," and about what needs to be studied (e.g., Berliner & Calfee, 1996, along with many other handbooks). But the most difficult problem confronting K-12 schooling today remains the American dilemma—the task of ensuring equal educational opportunities and outcomes for all students, regardless of background circumstances. We still have much to learn about formulating and understanding this problem, and about appropriate methodologies for investigating it.

The *NCLB* answer seems overly simple. First, developing dramatically effective strategies will depend on creative approaches for changing a system that has proven remarkably resistant to innovation. Before "proving" the large-scale effectiveness of programmatic alternatives, these need to be created and tried out in small-scale settings. As Pearson (in press) notes, advances in medicine come not from field trials, but from significant investments in fundamental and preliminary investigations; the experience resembles a rollercoaster ride more than a frontal assault (Calfee, Norman, Miller, Wilson, & Trainin, in press).

Given an adequate "front end" from which to move further, then what criteria apply in developing evaluation studies to assess the practicalities of implementing a particular program? Answering this question will center on **validity** issues, and the task of defending the meaning of the outcomes of an investigation (or collection of investigations). Research shows that Treatment A produces an advantage of a particular size compared with a control condition. The "obvious" interpretation is that this advantage will hold across a variety of settings and contexts; the finding will generalize. But what if the treatment is modified, accidentally or otherwise? What about interactions with different settings, populations, and times? What about the long-term impact of the treatment? What about transfer from proximal to distal outcomes, which might be more significant? Such questions "threaten" the interpretive validity of an investigation.

The construct of **control** refers to techniques used to address threats to interpretive validity. Creation of generalizable designs is an essential strategy for establishing adequate control. Those factors that may contribute to unsystematic variance and interactions are identified and incorporated in the design—factors related to program variations, implementation contexts, demographic characteristics, and outcomes short- and long-term, proximal and distal. Randomization does not provide systematic control, and may even be a digression.

In high school science, students learn "proper" methodology. Follow the prescribed procedures (it helps to come up with the right answer), and you will receive a high mark. Authentic research is more complex, requiring a blend of hard work, creative thought, and serendipity. The task is especially challenging in field settings. The theoretical and pragmatic efforts behind the Tacoma Narrows Bridge and Hormone Replacement Therapy were, by all appearances, of exceptional quality. But the bridge fell and the therapy has proved dangerous. The key to science is challenge; "Science is demarcated from nonscience by the fact that its hypotheses are, in principle, falsifiable, ... [and so] what counts is whether or not our conjecture survives a strenuous effort to refute it" (Phillips 2000). *NCLB* rests on the notion of "proven practice;" if a program developer obtains statistical significance, then the program is proven. From the scientific perspective, "What works" is an invitation for critical review and analysis.

Another item in the scientific enterprise centers around matters of theory, mechanisms, and "causes." The last mentioned is especially complex. *NCLB* advocates frequently claim that the randomized field experiment is both necessary and sufficient to establish causality. The rationale for this claim is unclear. As many philosophers of science have noted, establishing cause-effect relations requires more than empirical findings. Kincaid (1996) provides an elegant portfolio for establishing and defending causal claims. In general, empirical correlations provide weak support for causality. More convincing are theories of intervening mechanisms.

A messy practical point—random assignment of students to "treatments" in public schools is impractical and probably unethical. The impracticality is obvious. Imagine that parents are properly informed about an experiment in which their children will randomly be assigned to schools or teachers. They may not be told about the treatment conditions, unless their children are also prohibited from talking about "What happened in school today?" Federal regulations require informed voluntary consent and confidentiality, which Reyna worries might be "the undoing of the progress toward science enshrined in *NCLB*." Perhaps, but changing these policies is likely to be challenged for ethical reasons.

An alternative to random assignment of students is random assignment at other levels—teacher/classroom units, schools, districts, or event states. The problem with this strategy is the loss of statistical power and the consequent increase in costs. Statistical analyses reflect the unit of analysis. A study that compares an experimental treatment of Los Angeles schools with San Jose schools may involve hundreds of schools, thousands of teachers, and tens of thousands of students. Practically speaking, however, the project provides one degree of freedom (confounded at that) for statistical purposes (Coalition for Evidence-Based Policy, 2003), and the results will be difficult to interpret. If only states and districts and schools and classes and teachers and students were like peas in pods in pods.

THE PREPARATION OF EDUCATIONAL RESEARCHERS

Because Reyna offers rather strong comments in this arena, and because I have committed time to the business, I feel compelled to offer a few remarks. The first relies on anecdote, to be sure. Reyna suggests that research universities may be reluctant to hire "researchers" to serve as deans in colleges and schools of education. Based on my admittedly personal experience, one can clearly find exceptions to this claim. More to the point, my assessment of the individuals holding decanal positions in top-ranked educational units is quite positive regarding their research credentials.

But I do share the concern about how to recruit, prepare, and support the next generation of researchers, who must lead path-breaking investigations of the educational enterprise. What should they know? Who should they be? How should they be prepared? Why should they enter the field?

What should the next generation of educational researchers know? A simple answer emphasizes technical competence—design and analysis of experimental-control evaluations, for instance. For the past several years, the Spencer Foundation has pursued this question, and we can only hope to learn the results fairly soon. Meanwhile, the NRC report provides convincing guidelines. They need experience with a broad range of conceptual and technical skills and knowledge. The continuing debate about qualitative versus quantitative methods has proven counterproductive for a variety of reasons, and they need to "get over it." They need to understand that methodology should be determined by the shape of the problem.

Who should they be? Reyna offers important observations about this question. She notes that educational researchers span the range from academics to district-level evaluators to practitioners (teachers, educational specialists, and so on). So how to manage recruitment and certification? Reyna suggests that "locals" need to know more about research. To be sure, more is needed than science-appreciation if principles of evidence-based inquiry are to make their way into classroom practice (Calfee & Wilson, in press). But imagine that every district and school were responsible for bona fide local evaluation of educational programs, to determine "what works" within local contexts and implementation procedures. To be sure, accomplishing this goal would be a challenge; in California, district-level personnel who are responsible for research and evaluation often hold masters degrees, which may not prepare them for scientific investigations.

How should they be prepared? The answer depends in part on who they are. Education is a professional field, and so must attend to the practical aspects of the field. But let me turn again to the reasoning and procedures that undergird the scientific enterprise. My experience suggests that candidates for graduate work in education may not have been well served by high school science courses, and often bring a sense of advocacy. They are convinced of the merits of this or that principle or practice, and want to produce findings that support this conviction. Engagement with a problem or a hypothesis is certainly a necessary starting point. But science is about subjecting ideas and results to withering criticism. Showing that a particular program "works" in one setting is, at best, the beginning of the job of determining the conditions under which it *does not* work. And so the preparation of educational researchers should emphasize problem identification and formulation, the capacity to design and contextualize, skills for bringing a variety of methods into the picture, and the ability to construct and demolish evidence-based arguments; Shavelson and Towne (2002) provide the syllabus. Specialization is necessary, but the capacity to communicate across boundaries is equally essential. Unfortunately, educational researchers often form enclaves, and especially problematic is the separation between the academy and the field of practice, which may explain why many practitioners see little of value in research.

Why become an educational researcher? Promises of wealth and prestige seem unlikely, compared with alternatives inside and outside academia. "Follow the money" may seem harsh, but the funding for educational research is minuscule and uncertain, and at the federal level subject to numerous and changeable constraints. IES has proposed more reliance on peer review, which would be a welcome shift. But Reyna's paper suggests that the "peers" should not be chosen from the ranks of educational researchers. As someone who made the shift into education from another discipline, the notion of interdisciplinary collaboration makes sense, but that does not begin by stereotyping others.

FEDERAL ROLES IN PUBLIC SCHOOLING\

Reyna argues that past problems have been remedied by *NCLB*. Mandates for districts and schools, the institution of randomized field trials as a requirement for program certification, and the shifting of research funds to privilege certain forms of research (and certain researchers) will revolutionize the public school system in a matter of years. A review of recent history suggests that this view may be somewhat optimistic. But beyond the question of practicality, *should* the federal government use its leverage to mandate a national program for public schools of this magnitude and influence? The answer to this question does not rest on science, of course. Nor should it depend on "results," especially when the relevant outcomes are also determined by federal fiat. The answer rests on values and politics. *NCLB* sprang forth as a bipartisan effort, a centralized effort to influence local policy and practice. Local voices, especially those confronting the daunting challenges of the achievement gap, have been muted. One of our nation's values, enshrined in the Constitution, has to do with local autonomy. To be sure, certain problems transcend the capacity of the local community; poverty falls into this category, which would seem to justify federal programs addressing this issue. It is less clear to me that we have reached a point that requires federal control of the schools—especially in the absence of significant efforts to alleviate the substantial inequities in the resources available for public education. *NCLB* appears to be silent on this matter.

REFERENCES

Berliner, D. C., & Calfee, R. C. (Eds.) (1996). *Handbook of educational psychology.* New York: Macmillan.

Bond, G. L., & Dykstra, R. (1967). The cooperative research program in first-grade reading instruction. *Reading Research Quarterly, 2* (Whole).

Calfee, R. C., & Wilson, K. M. (in press). A classroom-based writing assessment framework. In C. A. Stone, E. R. Silliman, B. J. Ehren, & K. Apel (Eds.), *Handbook of language and literacy development and disorders.* New York: Guilford.

Calfee, R. C., Norman, K., Miller, R. G., Wilson, K., & Trainin, G. (in press). Learning to do educational research. In R. J. Sternberg & M Constas (Eds.), *Translating theory and research into practice.* Mahwah NJ: Lawrence Erlbaum Associates.

Cazden, C. B. (1988). *Classroom discourse: The language of teaching and learning.* Portsmouth NH: Heinemann.

Coalition for Evidence-based Policy. (2003). *Identifying and implementing educational practices supported by rigorous evidence: A user-friendly guide.* Washington DC: Institute for Educational Sciences.

Cronbach, L. J., & Suppes, P. (Eds.). (1969). *Research for tomorrow's schools: Disciplined inquiry for education.* New York: Macmillan.

Heath, S. B. (1983). *Ways with words.* New York: Cambridge University Press.

Kincaid, H. (1996). *Philosophical foundations of the social sciences.* New York: Cambridge University Press.

Lagemann, E. C., & Shulman, L. S. (Eds.). (1999). *Issues in education research: Problems and possibilities.* San Francisco: Jossey-Bass.

Pearson, P. D. (2004). The reading wars: The politics of reading research and policy—1988 through 2003. *Educational Policy, 18*(1), 216-252.

Phillips, D. C. (2000). *The expanded social scientist's bestiary: A guide to fabled threats to and defenses of, naturalistic social science.* New York: Rowman & Littlefield.

Stallings, J. (1975). Implementation and child effects of teaching practices in Follow Through classrooms. *Monographs of the Society for Research in Child Development, 40* (Serial No. 163).

CHAPTER 5

THE EDUCATION ACTS

Political Practice Meets Practical Problems, Scientific Processes, Process Control, and Parkinson's Law

Earl Hunt

Valerie Reyna (2004) has done us all a service by calling attention to the assumptions, intentions, and positive actions taken in two recent legislative acts, the *No Child Left Behind* and the *Education Science Reform* acts, to be referred to here collectively as The Education Acts. The Education Acts are based on two assumptions. The first is that education's highest priority is assuring an adequate level of basic skills in students toward the bottom end of the distribution of academic achievement, especially in the early school years. The argument for doing so is that children who fail to grasp the basics in elementary school will be unable to benefit from instruction in more advanced topics, especially in science and technology. The second is that educational reform should be based upon sound scientific evidence. This assumption is at least partly based on the belief that providing more federal money for education has not worked in the past,

The No Child Left Behind *Legislation:*
Educational Research and Federal Funding, 57–76
Copyright © 2005 by Information Age Publishing
All rights of reproduction in any form reserved.

and will not work again unless more care is taken about how the money is spent. A codicil to the assumption about the need for sound scientific evidence, which is unstated in the act but which Reyna certainly makes explicit in her article, is that a great deal of money was spent on activities that were fundamentally flawed, because they had been adopted without adequate scientific research.

The decision to emphasize basic skills and the early years was reasonable, although not inevitable. International comparisons of school achievement have consistently shown that during the early school years American schools do pretty well. The disparity between the achievements of the American and most foreign students widens in the middle school and high school years. One can argue that this is because the seeds of low accomplishment have been planted in American students during the early school years. The authors of the Education Acts probably thought that this was the case. On the other hand, it might be that the problem is with the middle and high school educational systems, and the social system within which they are embedded. The priority set forth in the Education Acts is not the only priority a reasonable person might have, but it is a reasonable priority in itself.

In any case, priority setting is a policy decision, we live in a democracy, and the policy decision has been made. This does not mean that research should be directed only at low achievers and basic skills, but it does establish a priority. Furthermore, as Reyna points out, this priority is sensible for the long-term nurturance of high achievers, especially in science and mathematics because, if it is successful, the reform program may attract students who are either economically disadvantaged or in demographic groups who are now underrepresented in rigorous scientific, engineering, and mathematical programs. I do not think any interested person would argue against the desirability of this goal.[1]

The second assumption of the Education Acts, that effective educational reform must depend upon good scientific research, is virtually independent of the first. One could make the case for scientific research in education if one's sole goal were the nurturance of potential Nobel laureates, to be selected from the presently best-educated strata of society!

No one would argue against the abstract proposition that educational reform should take advantage of good scientific research. This statement is akin to the "amen" after a prayer. The twin assertions that lack of science has crippled past attempts at reform and that reliance on science will more or less automatically improve science in the future are more arguable. It is certainly true that past educational efforts have not placed U.S. education where most of us want it to be. However it is not clear that this is because prior educational reform efforts were bad ideas in themselves. The problem may have been with their implementation.

The educational system does not operate in a vacuum. It is nurtured by, and constrained by, other forces in the society. For instance, educational reforms are almost all focused on what happens in the classroom and the school. The effectiveness of education may be constrained by parental and peer-group attitudes toward education and by social and economic conditions in the community. These constraints can be sufficiently strong to negate the effect of appropriate educational reforms, regardless of whether or not they are based upon good scientific research.

These arguments should be read as qualifications of Reyna's arguments and the assumptions in the Education Acts, not as objections to them. The priorities set forth in the acts are reasonable ones. We just want to be sure that in achieving them we do not unduly weaken our attempts to achieve other reasonable goals. Science has proven the best way to choose actions in many other fields, so it certainly is reasonable to apply scientific reasoning to educational reform. However it would be naïve to believe that an educational reform will succeed solely because it is built on a good scientific base. The step of translating scientific findings into action, the discipline of educational engineering, if you will, is every bit as important as the education sciences. The rest of this article is a hopefully constructive critique describing what I think needs to happen if we are to realize improvements in education through science.

TURNING HOTHOUSE SCIENCE INTO CONTINUED PRACTICE: THE SCALING UP PROBLEM

Reyna emphasizes the creation of a national clearinghouse, to serve as a repository of good ideas about education, all properly founded in scientific research. While the idea is useful in itself, it has a disturbing resemblance to the injunction "If you build it, they will come." "They," here, are the teachers and administrators responsible for the day-to-day activities in our nation's classrooms. There is an analogy here to the public library. Building the library is only half the task. The next half is to make sure that the information it contains is not only accurate, but is perceived to be both accurate and useful.

History is not encouraging. It is not too far off the mark to say that past educational research efforts, often backed by good scientific reasoning, can be characterized in the following way.

1. A granting agency gives some very smart, hardworking people a lot of money to build a new educational program.
2. The very smart people recruit a group of motivated teachers, who try out the new program. This usually requires extra work by the

teachers, so they are compensated, either with extra money or by relief from other duties.

3. Appropriate statistical evaluations show that the program either unequivocally worked or, at the least, is worth exploring further. However,

4. The money is now spent, so the very smart people go on to other things. The teachers go back to their normal practices, and

5. Education continues as if the project had never existed.

Steps 1–3 find out what educators should do. Steps 4–5 show that there are blocks to doing it. While we could always use better educational research, that research will be ineffective unless much more attention has been paid to the translation step, in which good ideas are incorporated into educational practice.

In education this is called the "scaling up" problem. It is at once time-consuming, expensive, and subject to a number of constraints due to the nature of our educational system. Nevertheless, the problem has to be solved if there is any hope for achieving educational reform, as opposed to publishing articles in a journal like this one.

In order to understand the problem it is useful to look at how an analogous problem has been handled in another section of our society, the much-maligned, but effective, military-industrial complex. The Department of Defense sponsors a great deal of research, both within and outside of its own laboratories. There is a continuum of research activities, ranging from the "pure" research activity associated with agencies such as the Office of Naval Research, much of which takes place in the university sector, to various applied laboratory programs, in which scientists within the military-industrial complex itself are asked to support the mission of operational, training, logistical, and planning commands. There are many conferences and workshops featuring presentations by people who work at various stages ranging from pure research to uses of new weapons, logistical, and personnel systems.

Pure researchers who work in the military-industrial system, in the university and elsewhere, do not spend much time talking to battalion commanders! Pure researchers do talk to people who talk to people who talk to battalion commanders. There are funds available to encourage joint projects along every link in the chain. No one, including Defense officials, would claim that the channel of information *and funding* for translation from the laboratory to the field is perfect. It exists, and it is big enough and good enough to be important.

The analogous channel for educational research is almost nonexistent. There are sporadic efforts to create something like it. The most notable one is probably the Bill and Melinda Gates Foundation's attempt to fund demonstration projects in systemwide reform. The success of such efforts, including widespread adoption of new methods by other districts and schools that did not receive special funding, has been at best spotty. Why?

There is no one reason. I can at best remark on a few of the obstacles that I have observed. The first is an excessive reliance on the "build it and they will come" mentality. As I have indicated, the modal educational experiment involves experiments with selected teachers. At this point the experimenters are usually in close touch with the classroom, extra support is often provided, and there are frequent exchanges between teachers and researchers concerning what is and what is not working.

The next step is to scale up to situations in which teachers are given (often minimal) instruction, the teachers are not made to feel that they are special in any way (because they are not), and the researchers have little if any control over the classroom. The innovation will not be implemented in as neat a way as it was in the controlled (and funded) classrooms, and results are often much less than had been hoped. At this point researchers report that "the method is only effective when implemented properly," and teachers and school administrators often cease their efforts—especially if the program entails expenses that are not covered by grant budgets.

Finding a way around this step is crucial. Furthermore, it is expensive. Let us look again at military and industrial practice. The military and industrial systems provide money for Research *and* Development, i.e., R & D. Training methods, new equipment, and new tactics are not expected to come out of the research laboratory ready to go. A prolonged development phase is expected. It is also expected to cost more than the research phase and often to take at least as long.

In spite of using the term R & D in some laboratory and center titles, developments in education-relevant sciences are too often describable as R & D efforts, with development tacked on to the last year of a 3- to 5-year grant. The development period should be much longer, should be better funded, and it probably should not be the responsibility of the granting agency. Adequate development requires a commitment from the receiving agencies, here school districts and statewide school systems, as much as it requires a push from the agencies responsible for the original product design.

A second problem is the looseness of the system. Military and industrial systems are characterized by a chain of command. In education the appropriate term may be a thread of suggestion. Let us look at how this affects the dissemination of research findings.

Development in the military-industrial complex is a fairly centralized operation. New systems are tried out using either experimental centers or operating units, the results are fed back to the laboratory, and the systems are redesigned and tried out again. Brigade and battalion commanders are expected to participate in such efforts, but they are not expected to pay for them. In the school system, though, it is not clear who is responsible for development. Research programs, such as the National Science Foundation's Research on Learning and Education (NSF-ROLE) program, certainly are not responsible for supporting the Wheresitat School District's implementation of a new reading program. The Wheresitat district superintendent is unlikely to have the funds to do the fine-tuning; Wheresitat can accept a program that has been proven "ready to go" elsewhere, but where is elsewhere? There is no guarantee that the fine-tuning required within the Wheresitat district will be the same as the fine-tuning needed in some other district, nor are there clear channels by which developmental findings at Wheresitat can be channeled to other districts.

From the viewpoint of state and district superintendents, educational researchers provide interesting ideas that might work in their own district or state, provided that the program is modified to fit local needs and capabilities. The superintendent has to ask two questions. They are "What benefit can this program achieve?" and "Who pays for the modifications and evaluations needed to move from laboratory to field?" The questions are not asked in the order that I have presented them. Because of the extremely tight economics of state and local funding, the cost question will be asked first. If it does not have an answer the value question will be of only passing interest.

When sources of state and local permanent funding are tightly constrained the cost question will not have an answer. Continuing the analogy to the Department of Defense, developmental funds are administered centrally, with selected field units being "asked" (more likely told) to assist in the evaluation phase. The U.S. Department of Education does not begin to have the degree of control found in Ministries of Education in most other industrial countries. Therefore there is no "central authority" that can fund field trials and insist upon the cooperation of operating units. This situation will almost certainly continue. We will not see a Ministry of Education in the near future; our traditions of state and local control are far too strong. (And a Ministry of Education brings its own problems.) The crunch on state and local funding will probably continue. This leaves development funding up in the air. Some way has to be found to bring it down to earth.

In addition to the funding problem there are two other obstacles to making the move from educational research to practice. A failure in the analogy between educational and military R&D helps us understand the first. The military does not move weapons, logistics, or communication systems directly from the laboratory to the battlefield. Soldiers fight using the methods and equipment with which they are familiar. New techniques are phased in, by conducting training and simulated battles with units who are not in contact with the real enemy.

The concept of being "out of the battle line" does not apply to education. Every teacher has real students, and those students are not to be experimented with lightly. I am not talking about "human subjects" considerations here, although I will get to that issue at the end of this essay. My point is that introducing a new teaching technique for, say, understanding the water cycle to one or two classes, is one thing. Introducing, for developmental purposes, a districtwide system for teaching biology is quite another. Yet that is just the sort of experimentation that is needed in order to bring teaching methods from the hot-house classroom of the dedicated teacher, assisted by researchers, to the colder, grimmer classroom of the average teacher who must implement a new method without ever meeting its developer.

The second obstacle has to do with the evaluation of a developmental effort. Some developmental efforts are going to be good ideas and some are going to be bad ones. Finding out which ones are which, and equally importantly, finding out how the research findings must be modified to be effective in practice, are not easy tasks. Part of the problem is bureaucratic. Machiavelli observed that those who wish to introduce innovation should not expect to be greeted joyfully by those who are doing well in the old system. There is an understandable conservatism in trying out new programs, because, as I have indicated, the "experimental subjects" will now be real children, to whom the school system has a real responsibility. This is combined with the fact that teachers and administrators in school systems appear to be incredibly busy. I own a pad of sticky notes with the slogan "I'm too busy mopping up the floor to turn off the faucet." I suggest that this problem is endemic throughout the educational system. The time pressures that all operational personnel feel, from superintendents to teachers, constitute a formidable barrier to innovation.

Paradoxically, the opposite error can also occur. As Reyna points out, the education system has sometimes suffered from the too-rapid acceptance of ideas or programs that have little concrete evidence behind them. Another military analogy is apt; in the Pentagon there is a saying that no weapons system was ever cancelled once the people associated with the program had their coffee mugs emblazoned with the program name. Education has certainly known the same thing; ideas that appeal to certain political or social desires can become the revealed wisdom even though their passage through the research phase was brief at best.

Such a charge requires a specific, so I will offer one. Everyone seems to believe in the importance of matching instruction to a student's learning style. This belief contains the implicit assumption that individual students have stable learning styles that they take from situation to situation, rather than altering their style to suit the current problem. The research demonstrating the existence of such traits is weaker than one would think it is from the sloganeering. I am not (here) arguing that learning styles do not exist. I just point out that the idea has received more credence than the evidence warrants. Similarly, educators regularly downplay the importance of "general intelligence." Yet the evidence for the concept is massive, if not politically correct. When it comes to development, advocates of a program have a powerful incentive to tell policy makers what they want to hear.

How, then, should a developmental effort be evaluated? The Education Acts, as summarized by Reyna, suggest that the evaluation be by scientific principles. In the abstract, who could be against this? But in the concrete, there are problems. Large-scale developmental efforts: (a) cannot be conducted in laboratory situations; and (b) should not be. In an excellent book on Decision and Judgment, Hammond (1996) pointed out that in the social sciences the tighter the control, the stronger the logical argument for a conclusion in the situation in which it was tested. That is what controlled experimentation is all about. On the other hand, the tighter the experimenter's control over the situation, the more likely it is that the resulting knowledge does not generalize, because the researchers kept out of the laboratory some variable that exerts a compelling, uncontrollable influence in the field.

Like parental attitudes toward education? Or union rules on teacher compensation and evaluation?

This brings me to my second concern, i.e., the Education Acts' almost touching reliance on the scientific method, as it is perceived by nonscientist policy makers and also, I fear, by too many educational researchers.

SCIENCE BY THE BOOK: STRESSING PROCESS OVER PRINCIPLES

The Education Acts properly emphasize the importance of solid scientific research on educational topics. By doing so, legislators took three steps forward. The legislators then took one and a half steps backward. They defined science in the legalistic manner to which legislators are accustomed. In doing so they confused the essence of science with its surface aspects. The confusion is serious because if these criteria are written into the project review process creative educational researchers are going to be severely limited.

The essence of science is an appeal to observation as the arbiter of truth, rather than relying on appeals to personal belief, faith, or ideology.

In order to make sense of observation scientists have devised a variety of methodologies and procedures for social control, ranging from statistical analysis through the use of hypothesis testing, and on to peer review. These techniques are useful processes in science, but they must not be confused with science itself.

The distinction between scientific reasoning and the processes used to support such reasoning is important. In the social sciences an initial stage of systematic observation may be required before hypotheses are to be tested. This is especially true in the developmental stage. You can be almost certain that when a new instructional method, properly evaluated by educational research, is "scaled up" something will go wrong. Systematic, possibly expensive, observation is essential. The same thing is often true of the first stage of a research project. It would be nice if researchers could simply take an existing theory from cognitive psychology and apply it directly to the improvement of learning. In fact, careful, systematic, well-recorded observation will probably be required first, in order to understand precisely how cognitive theory is supposed to fit into different classrooms. Failure to do this can result in either premature rejection of a good theory or, worse, the reduction of theory to inanities such as "students must interact with the material and concepts of a class."

Is this a serious problem? The following story suggests that it is. In October of 2003 the National Science Foundation (NSF) Research on Learning and Education (ROLE) program convened a principal investigator's meeting that featured Russell Hulse, a Nobel Laureate in Physics, as a keynote speaker. Hulse described the course of his research on binary pulsars, the studies for which he was awarded the prize. He pointed out that initially he had not been looking for binary pulsars at all; he had been involved in the systematic recording of ordinary pulsars in an unexplored section of the sky. During this recording he encountered a very small number of pulsars that behaved in an unusual way. (Educational researchers might have rejected these observations as being statistically insignificant.) Only then did he construct a model. He next showed that the model generated equations that described the data, but he never "tested a hypothesis" comparing his theory to some other theory. He never had a control group, for the idea was irrelevant.

Hulse made a point of the fact that he had not done science by the book. To the credit of the NSF staff, one of the ROLE program directors stood up and said, with his tongue not entirely in his cheek, that if Hulse had been an education researcher his proposal would not have been funded. Amplifying, I do not believe Hulse's initial investigations would have fit the Education Acts definition of science. There is something wrong here.

Exactly the same argument can be applied to the Education Acts' emphasis on "peer-reviewed papers in solid journals." Peer review is certainly a good thing. However passing (or failing) peer review means, operationally, that two or three individuals with reasonably appropriate backgrounds either did or did not agree with the author. That is not an infallible way to screen for truth.

More generally, ideas stand up on their own. Some of the most influential research in the cognitive sciences and in education rests substantially on reports in books or edited collections of papers. When a review committee evaluates a proposal they can and should, legitimately, ask for papers supporting the ideas contained in the proposal. They, the reviewers, should then decide if whether or not the evidence presented in the papers is adequate. This decision is to be made by reading and analyzing the papers. The reviewers are responsible themselves for making such evaluations. Yielding their judgment to the two or three unknown peer reviewers, or refusing to consider an idea because the paper in which it appeared was not peer-reviewed, is an abdication of responsibility.

I am certainly not arguing against hypothesis testing, controlled experimentation, or peer review. They are all highly useful processes that often result in good scientific products. I return to the basic point. The core of scientific reasoning is the evaluation of ideas against data. That is sacrosanct. The authors of the Education Acts are to be applauded for stressing this. Where they erred was in trying to define the processes by which scientific reasoning advances. The processes they identified are a reasonable subset of possible processes, but no more than that. Legislative proscription of the way science is to be done is a very bad idea.

I point out that I am not alone in trying to distinguish between the logic of science and the processes of doing science. A National Academy report on science in education research (Shavelson & Towne, 2002) reached much the same conclusion I have, yet it seems to have had relatively little effect on the legalistic approach to science taken both in the Education Acts and, I am afraid, by some granting agencies.

These remarks are directed at the way that educators should think about science, and especially the three areas of science most relevant to education; developmental, cognitive, and differential psychology. We may turn the critique around. Reyna wants more educators to be educated in these three branches of psychological science. Is this a good idea?

It was, but it may not be in the future. All three of these areas of psychology are now being heavily influenced by major developments in the neurosciences. There is some truth to the advice that if you want to get a grant, you do not call yourself a cognitive psychologist, you call yourself a cognitive neuroscientist. This movement has already produced, and will produce in the future, major advances toward the goal of connecting psychological behavior to brain structures and mechanisms. That is a good thing. What this trend means for education is a bit more problematical.

Bruer (2003) has referred to attempts to anchor educational psychology in the neurosciences as "a bridge too far." My view, which closely parallels Bruer's, is that in the majority of situations, educators have to deal with students as cognitive and social beings, with their biology being only of passing interest. Educators require sciences of cognition that deal with such things as the influence of belief structures upon the acceptance of scientific ideas, ways in which environmental variables can enhance young children's ability to pay attention, or how social structures reinforce or inhibit learning when students work in groups. Elsewhere (Hunt, 2002) I have referred to such concerns as thinking at the representational and information processing levels. That is where education takes place; educators influence students by presenting arguments and making sure that students have certain experiences. Except in a very few situations, education does not rely on physiological interventions.

In order to influence thinking at the representational and information processing levels educators require a theory of cognition that deals with variables at these levels, rather than one that explains how the primitive mechanisms of thought arise from brain mechanisms. The present move from cognitive and developmental psychology to cognitive and developmental neuroscience is not irrelevant to the construction of such a theory. The more closely psychological theories are related to neuroscientific findings, the more likely the psychological theories are to be right. This, alone, is not enough. If psychological findings are to be relevant to education they have to make contact with the sorts of variables that educators deal with; behavior, not neural impulses or fMRI indicators of brain metabolism.

To the extent that psychology's rush to the neurosciences inhibits the development of behavioral theories of learning, social cognition, intelligence, and problem solving the discipline of psychology will become decreasingly relevant to education. Perhaps educational psychology departments themselves can be strengthened to fill the gap. Perhaps we will see the rise of departments of behavioral psychology that provides bridges between the neurosciences and both educational and engineering disciplines. It is hard to see far into the future. What we can see, though, is the problem on the horizon.

ASSESSMENT: GOOD! PROCESS CONTROL: GOOD! ACCOUNTABILITY: MAYBE NOT SO GOOD!

The Education Acts place great stress on educational assessment. Both in the acts and in commentaries about them, assessment is linked closely to accountability. The emphasis is slightly off the mark.

Accountability is a legal concept. Holding someone accountable for something implies three things; that something bad happened, that the person being held accountable had the knowledge and power to keep the bad thing from happening, and that they did not act appropriately. In education these implications are often false. Teachers, in particular, may not know how well their students are doing. Teachers and administrators often do not have either the training or the power to change some of the major constraints on their student's performance. These facts do not mean that assessment should be dropped. They do mean that we should think of educational assessment in another way.

Assessment in education should be thought of as a means to achieve quality control, not legal accountability. Quality control measures are intended to do two things: ensure that a product or service meets some minimum standard of acceptability and, beyond the minimum, to provide information that can be used to build a better product or service. It is fairly easy to fulfill the first goal. All one has to do is to articulate the standards for minimum acceptability clearly, and to design measures relevant to these standards. This view of quality control is so close to the role that assessment is assigned in the education acts that I could be accused of playing with words. Any program that certifies individual students as having passed standards performs the acceptability test of quality control.

However if one wants to improve the system, the other goal, providing information to direct constructive change, is far more useful. Assessment as it is currently being implemented, in "standardized tests," most emphatically does not meet this goal.

The sorts of assessments envisaged by the education acts have three important characteristics. The first is that they are "drop in from the sky" tests, in the sense that they are developed and largely administered by some body other than the body charged with education itself.[2] For instance, many of the tests are developed by commercial companies, acting as contractors to state authorities rather than local district authorities. In other cases the state administration itself develops the examination. State administrators, like the contractors are divorced from day-to-day contact with students. Because accountability is stressed, these tests understandably generate a good deal of anxiety. As a result, and inevitably, teachers will teach to the tests, insofar as they are able to do so. This creates two further complications.

In principle, teaching to a well-designed test is not a bad thing. The problem comes when the primary purpose of the test is to ensure that students are meeting minimum standards. I will refer to such tests as *certification* tests. Certification tests are intended to assure that students have an acceptable degree of skill or knowledge across a wide range of topics. Focussing on certification will encourage teaching that covers many topics in a shallow manner, rather than stressing substantial understanding of key principles in a few fields Because the tests are administered on a "drop in from the sky" basis, rather than being integrated into classroom practices, both the administration of a test and the preparation that teachers make for it will produce some disruption from regular instruction.

Part of this problem lies in the curriculum itself. It can be argued that American schools simply try to do too much. This is especially a problem in areas of science, technology, and, I believe to a lesser extent, mathematics. However a part of the problem is associated with the unfortunate combination of testing for certification with testing for quality control.

There is a good case for making testing for certification broad and shallow. On the other hand, testing for quality control requires fairly deep probing of different topics, ranging from writing and the social sciences to physics and biology. It is economically impossible to conduct such assessments by using a "drop in from the sky" examination that is taken by all students. The testing program would be far too expensive and would produce too much disruption in the teaching program.

"Drop in from the sky" testing could be used to conduct deep, probing examinations of the knowledge of randomly selected students, with different students being evaluated in different content areas. Such a program would provide very useful information about the state of education at the national, state, and possibly the district level. Indeed, the National Assessment of Educational Progress (NAEP) program comes close to being such a program. However programs like NAEP fail another important aspect of quality control, they do not provide rapid feedback at the level of the school and the classroom.

Informative feedback is effective if it is prompt enough and specific enough so that the feedback can be linked to the actions that produced the feedback signal. Large "drop in from the sky" tests, graded by some entity outside of the school or classroom, inevitably provide very slow feedback. In many cases teachers will not learn how their students did on a statewide assessment test until sometime in the academic year after the test was taken. At this point the students are gone and the teacher has forgotten how the relevant lessons went. I believe that the hostility that many teachers have expressed toward standardized assessments is partly due to these deficiencies. The feedback they provide is too slow and too generalized to help in the improvement of instruction.

The problem of generalized feedback goes beyond telling the teacher how the students did. Informative feedback should be linked to some sort of advice to the teacher, not just telling the teacher that the students are performing at some level, but telling both teachers and students precisely how the learning process is going wrong, and suggesting ways that the teacher and student can work to improve learning. This is particularly the case in the American education system, for the teaching turnover rate is rather high. At any one time many of the teachers will have a rather small amount of classroom experience. The problem appears to be most severe in science and mathematics. The inexperienced teacher should look on student assessments as devices to help them improve, not devices to "hold them accountable."

Testing programs that could provide appropriate feedback have been developed. They are based on the computer driven, interactive technologies that are increasingly available in the classroom. This is not the place to describe the assessment programs in detail (but see Hunt & Pellegrino, 2002 and Pellegrino, Chudowsky, & Glaser, 2001 for a discussion of some examples.) These technology-heavy assessment systems integrate testing and instruction in a completely objective way and are far less disruptive of normal instruction than "drop in from the sky" testing. Feedback can be provided to the students within seconds (literally) of a response, and summary feedback can be provided to teachers as rapidly as they want it. One can envisage a data collection system that a state superintendent could use to monitor exactly what percentage of students had reached which level of standards in which subjects, on a daily or weekly basis.

One of the consequences of the Education Acts and the political events that lead up to them has been a rush to adopt "drop in from the sky" testing. There has been no great rush to adopt assessment integrated with learning. Sadly, there is a reason for this. Virtually all the techniques that integrate assessment with learning have been developed as research projects. Several of them are quite successful, by any reasonable standard. However, they do not provide the breadth of subject coverage that school systems need, nor have they been subjected to the large-scale field evaluations that are so necessary before they can be used to supplement and, eventually, to replace the sorts of assessment for accountability envisaged in the Education Acts.

Why are these research programs in such a state, after literally millions of education dollars have been spent developing them? I gave the reason earlier in the first stage of this essay. While we could always use more research on new assessment methods, what is really needed is development, to move present ideas into the practice of the near future. In the education system the D part of R & D has fallen squarely between the cracks separating state and federal responsibility.

THE ISSUE OF PARTICIPANT'S RIGHTS:
A SERIOUS CONCERN MEETS PARKINSON'S LAW

At the end of her paper Reyna expresses concern that the laws and regulations relating to protection of human subjects are inhibiting the development of a science-based system of education. I believe that almost everyone associated with educational research will agree.

Adequate research in the education sciences requires the observation of a wide range of activities, and observation on all the students and teachers in school systems, not just the biased samples that volunteer for experimental participation. We have to balance rights against risks. When "risk" is interpreted in a medical context it will take on a weight that is simply not proportional to the weight that it should have in most educational and behavioral research.

It must be admitted that educationists have, in a sense, asked for this situation by using medical terminology to describe their research programs: talking about "at risk populations" and "do no harm," when the medical analogy was strained at best. Perhaps the educationists hoped that the prestige and money of biomedical research would spill over into educational research. What happened, though, was that the biomedical regulations spilled over.

It is easy to fulminate, it is easy to complain, and, as one of my graduate student colleagues wisely pointed out to me, it is healthier to laugh at some of the irrelevant regulations imposed upon education researchers than it is to fume at them and risk a heart attack. From time to time I have both fumed and laughed. I will now attempt to be constructive.

The appropriate protection of the rights of participants in research is essential. From the viewpoint of the education researcher, though, society's decision to write laws and regulations protecting those rights arose in the context of medical research. The issue of protection in medical research is different from analogous issues in human research in two important ways. One are obvious, the other less so.

The risks arising from medical research can be very much greater than the risks associated with educational research. Educational research risks almost all revolve around questions of confidentiality of data, rather than exposure to physical risk. As a codicil, confidentiality in education has to include confidentiality not only for the obvious "subject," the student, but also for the teachers, curriculum designers, and administrators involved.

The primary "subjects" in educational research, K–12 students, are required to participate in the educational system itself. Furthermore, as a matter of practicality, most students have no choice about whether to participate or not, and only very limited choice in how they will participate. It can be argued, strongly, that because K–12 participation is involuntary the educational system has the obligation, not as an opportunity, but as a duty, to conduct research in order to improve the system. Educators dealing with the K–12 system owe this to their largely captive audience. Paradoxically, when the philosophy appropriate to participants' rights in medical research is applied the principle is turned around. Biomedical research assumes that the participant can always opt out of treatment. We have universal, compulsory education for a reason. That reason brings with it the duty to conduct research to make compulsory education better.

To appreciate this point, note that colleges and universities, by contrast, are morally free to choose to do or not do research to improve their educational product. Why? Students in higher education institutions can vote with their feet in a way that most K–12 students cannot. I, personally, am in favor of educational research on the higher education system, but I see this as a policy decision to improve the institution's position in the educational market place, rather than as a moral imperative.

The problem is to reconcile the requirement for research with a legitimate concern for the rights of research participants. This end is not being achieved very well today, because the ubiquitous Institutional Review Boards (IRBs) are charged with enforcing on behavioral and educational researchers a set of rules that were primarily written for medical research. In order to keep this problem to a minimum the writers of the national regulations included in them some exemptions and easing of regulation for behavioral and educational research. However IRBs (and most definitely the bureaucrats who support them) often interpret these exemptions easing of regulations very conservatively. Being somewhat jocular, it sometimes seems as if the IRBs and their bureaucrats believe that "when in doubt, assume that the research involves neurosurgery." Exemptions for what, to an interested layperson, would be educational research can be few and far between.

I do not think that this happens because IRB members and their bureaucrats are evil people. I think that it is due to two pervasive tendencies in our society. One is the concern for accountability, interpreted very much as it is interpreted when the educational acts discuss assessment. When something goes wrong, our legalistic society wants a clear record of accountability so that we know *whom* to blame. As I have already argued, it might be more productive to think of qualitative control, so that more things go right. At present, though, we are in a situation that stresses accountability in the legal sense. Accountability involves both rules and their interpretation. In the medical setting, IRBs and their bureaucrats are given little leeway in rule interpretation, because of the very severe nature of the problems that can exist when things go wrong. Behavioral and educational researchers then have to live with this attitude toward rule interpretation in situations where it is hard to imagine how anything very bad could happen.

The other pervasive tendency is a bureaucratic tendency known as Parkinson's Law. This "law" was first promulgated by C. Northcote Parkinson, a British political scientist and blessed with a biting wit. Parkinson's Law asserts that, "Work expands to fill the time available for its completion"

(Parkinson, 1957). A corollary to Parkinson's Law is that bureaucratic staffs expand continuously, independently of the need for their services.

There is more than a kernel of truth to this. Everyone believes that his or her function is important. In the case of the IRBs and their supporting bureaucrats this belief is correct. On the other hand, the IRBs and the bureaucrats have virtually no surveillance capability. Errors and violations are called to their attention, but they receive very little feedback concerning the costs they are imposing on researchers or the extent to which things are going right. Given the sorts of feedback that the IRBs and supporting bureaucracy get, it is understandable that they keep expanding their jurisdiction both by incorporating educational research into their purview and by promulgating local rules that actually go beyond the federal rules. Parkinson's law applies, not because the people involved are petty or evil, but because they are acting the way people act when placed in rule-making roles, divorced from knowledge about the costs their rules are creating.

I do not see how this situation can be cured as long as the ethical regulations for educational research are derived from those intended for biomedical research. Ethical regulations must remain; there is no question about that. What does not have to remain, though, is the tie to biomedical ethical regulation. The federal regulating power for non-biomedical research could be removed from the National Institutes of Health and given to an agency primarily concerned with funding of behavioral and educational research, such as the Department of Education or the education directorate of the National Science Foundation.

I recommend this with some trepidation, because it would mean the establishment of two lines of authority over human subjects, with the associated collection of IRBs and associated bureaucrats. There would inevitably be borderline cases, where jurisdiction was not clear. However the present system is adding to the expense and sometimes limiting the feasibility of important educational research. I think that this will continue as long as the same IRB system deals with both biomedical and behavioral research.

CONCLUSION

Policy makers are understandably frustrated when policy analysts offer critiques that seem like carping. Richard Nixon's Vice President, Spiro Agnew, described the press as "nattering nabobs of negativism." Few political leaders today would publicly associate themselves with Nixon and Agnew, because both resigned from political office in the face of charges of misconduct. Nevertheless, I suspect that many of our current policy makers think that Agnew had it right about the press, and he could have thrown in the professoriate for good measure. Can't we ever be pleased?

Reyna's basically positive view of the Education Acts contrasts with that of many educators, who have focused on problems and especially the requirements related to assessment and accountability. I think Reyna is correct. These acts are well intended, in the sense that they represent attempts to apply one of the most successful techniques of reasoning that our society has, scientific analysis, to a pressing social problem. This does not mean that the acts are perfect, and the question of whether or not the acts will be funded adequately is an entirely separate issue. The Education Acts have promise, but that this problem will not be realized, even if funds are forthcoming, unless structural changes are made.

Scientists who want to improve education cannot simply do studies, publish the results in journals, and expect educators to adopt the revealed wisdom. Some way has to be found to deal with the "scaling up" problem, what the military and industrial sectors would call Development after Research has been done. It will be very hard to deal with this problem because of the strong tradition of decentralization in American education. New organizational and funding structures may be needed. These will not be created overnight.

In addition to creating structures to link science to education, educators will have to find closer ways to improve the quality of scientific findings relevant to education. The Education Acts envisaged this, by emphasizing the need to root proposed innovations in established scientific findings. In order to achieve this goal, two things must happen.

The most important is that educators (and funders of education!) must take a broader view of science. They too often think of science as a set of processes to be followed, rather than as a philosophical commitment to empirical observation as the arbiter of truth, with the processes of observation to be adjusted to the situation. In my opinion the process-oriented view of science has hurt educational innovation in the past, and if is perpetuated, it will stifle needed innovation in the future.

The other thing that has to happen is the scientists outside of the education system have to provide scientific models that are relevant to education. The onus here lies primarily upon cognitive and developmental psychologists, although sociology, anthropology, and economics are also relevant. The current move toward deriving psychology from the neurosciences, which is laudable in itself, must not inhibit the development of theories of human behavior that come to grips with the sorts of variables that educators can use to influence behavior.

The Education Acts assign a central role to assessment, but they do so primarily as a way to certify students as minimally educated, and as a way obtain accountability. Assessment is important, but the analogy to accountability in the legal sense is not. The correct analogy is to industrial quality control; assessment to improve the product rather than assessment to assign the blame. Once the quality control analogy is adopted the need for different forms of assessment, for different purposes, and the need to integrate assessment with learning both become apparent.

Suppose that we deal with these three major issues: the move from research to practice, the proper uses of science and assessment, and also make the administrative adjustments needed to retain appropriate human subjects safeguards without stifling needed research relevant to education. If these things happen the Education Acts may go down in history as a major step forward in American education. If we do not deal with these issues, and especially if we do not find better ways of moving from research to practice, the Acts will sink and be forgotten, as yet another example of political leaders trying to improve education, and then having their attention diverted before the job was done.

Time will tell.

NOTES

1. While no reasonable person would argue against the desirability of the goal of attracting more minority group members and women into science and mathematics, some might argue against its feasibility. Herrnstein and Murray (1994) and Jensen (1998) have both maintained that, even under the best of circumstances, the percentage of people who have the intellectual capability to perform at high levels is lower in minority groups than in the general population, and with respect to mathematical-spatial abilities, low in women. While their contention cannot be disproved by presently available data, the evidence does not prove it, either. And there is certainly no evidence to indicate that the disparity in talent, across groups, could not be corrected by better education. It is clearly both wise and humane to try.

2. I wish I could take credit for this term but I cannot. I first heard it used by Robert Mislevy, then at the Educational Testing Service.

REFERENCES

Bruer, J. T. (2003). Learning and technology: A view from cognitive science. In H. F. O'Neil, Jr., & R. S. Perez (Eds), *Technology applications in education: A learning view* (pp. 159–172). Mahwah, NJ: Lawrence Erlbaum Associates.

Hammond, K. R. (1996). *Human judgment and social policy: Irreducible uncertainty, inevitable error, unavoidable injustice.* Oxford, England: Oxford University Press.

Herrnstein, R. J., & Murray, C. (1994). *The Bell Curve: Intelligence and class structure in American Life.* New York: The Free Press

Hunt, E. (2002). *Thoughts on thought: A discussion of formal models of cognition.* Mahwah, NJ: Lawrence Erlbaum Associates.

Hunt, E., & Pellegrino, J. W. (2002). Issues, examples, and challenges in formative assessment. *New Directions for Teaching & Learning, 89,* 73–85.

Jensen, A. R. (1998). *The g factor: The science of mental ability.* Westport, CT: Praeger.

Parkinson, C. N. (1957). *Parkinson's law, and other studies in administration.* Boston: Houghton Mifflin.

Pellegrino, J. W., Chudowsky, N., &. Glaser, R. (Eds.). (2001). *Knowing what students know: The science and design of educational assessment.* Washington, DC: National Academy Press.

Reyna, V. (2005). The *No Child Left Behind Act* and scientific research: A view from Washington, DC. In J. S. Carlson & J. R. Levin (Eds.), *Scientifically-based education research and federal funding agencies: The case of the* No Child Left Behind *legislation* (Vol. 1, pp. 1-25). Greenwich, CT: Information Age.

Shavelson, R. J., & Towne, L. (Eds.). (2002). *Scientific research in education.* Washington, DC: National Academy Press.

CHAPTER 6

WHY CONVERGING SCIENTIFIC EVIDENCE MUST GUIDE EDUCATIONAL POLICIES AND PRACTICES

G. Reid Lyon

Valerie Reyna has provided an excellent contribution to the discussion of the need for educational policies and instructional practices to be firmly rooted in converging scientific evidence. Her analysis of the bipartisan *No Child Left Behind Act* (NCLB) and the *Education Sciences Reform Act* (ESRA) and their implications for student achievement, improvement in the quality of educational research, and the preparation of future educational researchers, practitioners, and educational leaders is timely and compelling. Her insights should be taken seriously not only because they are well informed and thoughtful but also because they were shaped by her experiences as an effective senior advisor to the U.S. Department of Education. In that role, she helped to craft the *ESRA* and other research initiatives currently supported by the Institute of Educational Sciences. While my response to Dr. Reyna's paper might be more interesting if I disagreed with the points she made, the fact is I do not. She has provided

The No Child Left Behind *Legislation:*
Educational Research and Federal Funding, 77–87
Copyright © 2005 by Information Age Publishing
All rights of reproduction in any form reserved.

an accurate summary of both *NCLB* and *ESRA* and the reasons for their development and subsequent passage into law. I will take this opportunity to provide additional background to the discussion with an eye toward explicating why the *No Child Left Behind Act* (and *Reading First* in particular) *and* an increased reliance on scientific research and "educational scientists" are critical for the educational well being of our nation's children.

NCLB AND *READING FIRST*

Dr. Reyna has appropriately pointed out that the sweeping educational policy changes presented in *NCLB* were not conceptualized and codified in legislation in a vacuum. For example, the specific need within *NCLB* for accountability for results and an increase in parental choice to find competent schools for their children was predicated on the simple fact that millions of children do not currently profit from their public education. This is particularly the case in the area of reading. Despite its critical importance, an unacceptable number of children cannot read proficiently. The National Center for Educational Statistics (NCES) recently reported that in the fourth grade alone, 37% of students read below the basic level nationally with only 31% of fourth-graders reading at the proficient level or above (NCES, 2003). If one disaggregates the national data by subgroup, over 60% of African American and over 50% of Hispanic/Latino students read below basic levels, with only 12 and 15% reading proficiently, respectively (NCES, 2003). This is appalling. To be clear, it is not race or ethnicity that gives rise to this significant underachievement in reading—it is poverty—and minority students happen to be over-represented among disadvantaged families.

Two additional facts underscore the reasons why accountability for results, state and local flexibility, parental choice, and evidence-based practices in education are the central programmatic "pillars" within *NCLB* and in the *Reading First* provisions within the legislation. First, the current trend in reading scores not only reflects an abysmal educational outcome, but a highly persistent one. As Reyna points out, NAEP reading scores at the fourth, eighth, and twelfth grades continue to show remarkably stagnant deficiencies in reading ability over the past 2 decades despite significant increases in educational funding. Second, and equally disconcerting, we now know that the majority of children *can* learn to read proficiently irrespective of their socioeconomic backgrounds if their reading instruction is grounded in, and informed by, the converging scientific evidence that helps explain (a) how reading skills develop; (b) why many children have difficulties; (c) how reading failure can be prevented; and (d) how reading difficulties, if not prevented, can be remediated (Lyon, 2002; Lyon et al., 2001; Shaywitz, 2003; Stanovich, 2000; Torgesen, 2002).

But given that substantial scientific evidence exists demonstrating that most reading failure can be either prevented or remediated provided that effective programs and interventions are implemented under the appropriate conditions, why has it taken so long for reading instruction to be informed by the evidence? In addition, why has it been necessary to forge federal policies to ensure that the instruction our children receive is predicated on scientific evidence of effectiveness? Finally, what is different about *NCLB*, and particularly *Reading First*, from earlier education legislation, that increases the probability that reading instruction will be genuinely linked to converging scientific evidence of effectiveness? I will address each of these questions in turn.

WHY THE GAP BETWEEN SCIENTIFIC RESEARCH AND READING INSTRUCTION?

There are a number of factors that have impeded the systematic use of scientific evidence to guide the development and implementation of educational policies, instructional programs, approaches, and/or strategies to foster proficient reading ability (see Lyon, Shaywitz, Chhabra, & Sweet, 2004). I will highlight three here. First, as Adams and Bruck (1995a, 1995b) point out, there was, and continues to be, a decided antiscientific spirit within the education profession in general, and within the reading research and practice communities, in particular. In the extreme, some members of the academic education establishment reject traditional scientific approaches to the study of reading development and instruction and support the perspective that the value of any evidence, scientific or not, is in the eye of the beholder. Specifically, truth is viewed as relative and framed via one's own experience and culture (Ellis & Fouts, 1997; McKenna, Stahl, & Reinking, 1994; Stanovich, 2000). Unfortunately, it is the case that many prospective and veteran teachers have been taught to discount the role of scientific research in informing them about reading development and instruction (Adams & Bruck, 1995a). Second, teachers are frequently confronted with confusing scientific jargon, combined with a lack of robust training in the principles of scientific research, making it difficult to discriminate between research findings that are valid and findings that are invalid (Kennedy, 1997). All too often teachers are asked to implement simplistic "magic bullet" solutions that are ostensibly "research-based" to increase student achievement only to find they fail. It is not surprising that many teachers have lost faith in the ability of research to inform their instructional practices. Third, it has been rare for policy makers at either the federal or state level to have a firm understanding of the role that scientific evidence can play in educational policy development and implementation. Even when there is recognition that scientific research is critical to other policy environments (e.g., public health, welfare reform, agriculture), education has typically been viewed as more value and guild driven. Thus, primary policy input is obtained from diverse special interest groups and politicians rather than educational scientists (Lyon & Chhabra, 2004; Lyon et al., 2004).

WHY THE NEED FOR *NCLB* AND *READING FIRST*?

To be blunt, if history serves, it is highly unlikely that educational policies and practices would change appreciably without linking federal education funding explicitly to accountability for results. Historically, the implementation of effective programs where instructional effectiveness is established through objective scientific analysis has not been part of the educational culture. Indeed, as Reyna points out, much of the previous policies and practices in education have focused little on student learning as a primary objective. For example, over the past 2 decades a major goal of reading instruction has been to foster a motivation and love for reading seemingly without the realization that learning to read is a necessary precursor to a love of reading (Lyon et al., 2004; Moats, 2000, Stanovich, 2000). It is indeed the case that most educational (to include reading) policies and instructional practices over the past century have been grounded in opinion, untested assumptions, ideology, philosophical positions, and political persuasions rather than in scientific evidence (McDaniel, Sims, & Miskel, 2001; Stanovich, 2000; Sweet, in press). And the effects of this practice are not only reflected in the number of educational fads foisted on teachers and children on a frequent basis but in the dismal results that such practices produce. Whether we like it or not, the persistence of ineffective philosophically and ideologically driven policies and practices is a stark testament to the immutability of the educational culture that reinforces instructional impotence, even in the presence of demonstrably more effective practices. *NCLB* and *Reading First* are legislative attempts to ensure that funding is available for instructional programs and professional development opportunities that are proven to be effective in helping children learn.

WHAT IS DIFFERENT ABOUT NCLB AND READING FIRST?
THE IDEA BEHIND THE READING FIRST PROGRAM

As Reyna explains, the development and implementation of the *Reading First* initiative within *NCLB* was built on: (a) the continued recognition that many of our nation's children, particularly those from disadvantaged environments continued to struggle in reading; (b) the continuing convergence of scientific evidence on reading development, reading difficulties, and effective reading instruction; (c) the need to increase the identification and implementation of reading and professional development programs based on scientific research; (d) the need to redefine the federal role in education by requiring all states to set high standards of achievement and to create a system of accountability to measure results; (e) the need to provide flexibility to states and local districts in meeting their specific needs; and (f) the need to significantly improve the federal and state grant application process and the federal and state *Reading First* monitoring process at the local (grantee) level in order to provide technical assistance where necessary and to terminate programs where necessary.

In order to achieve these goals, the *Reading First* initiative significantly increased the federal investment in scientifically based reading instruction in the early grades, and stressed accountability for results and a systematic monitoring and evaluation system to ensure fidelity of implementation of *Reading First* approved programs. Indeed, monitoring, evaluation, and capacity building are absolutely critical to the success of *NCLB* as was learned from earlier reading legislation. As Lyon et al. (2004) point out, earlier federal legislative attempts to ensure that all children were provided evidence-based instruction as seen for example in the *Reading Excellence Act (REA)*, were, in essence, ineffective for several reasons. For example, while initial federal review of state *REA* grant applications provided quality control over the criteria that states would employ to assure that instructional and professional development programs were based upon scientific research, the states did not implement these standards in a systematic manner. Moreover, the federal government underestimated the resistance within the local districts' reading communities to the implementation of scientifically based reading programs. Indeed, site visits to many states indicated that ineffective reading programs in use before *REA* funding were still in use and supported through *REA* funds, irrespective of their scientific underpinnings. Finally, the experience with the *REA* indicated significant gaps in state, local, and school level understanding of scientifically based reading programs as well as the need for increased professional development at the university, state, and district levels to support the implementation of acceptable reading programs and approaches.

Given this background, it was clear that any increase in student reading achievement produced by *Reading First* would happen if, and only if, the U.S. Department of Education developed and put in place programmatic policies and procedures to ensure successful implementation. Within this context, the probability of children benefiting from the *Reading First* (and

Early Reading First) programs is significantly increased by the following factors:

Substantial Increase in Funding for Reading First—Approximately 1 billion dollars per year for a 6-year period is being provided to eligible states and local school districts for the implementation of instructional programs based on scientifically based reading research (SBRR). This substantial funding increase over previous programs is also based, in part, on data indicating that investment in high quality reading instruction at the K–3 levels could help to reduce the number of children requiring later special education services for reading failure (President's Commission on Excellence in Special Education, 2002).

Strong Statute—The *Reading First* grant program states clearly that all program activities must be based on SBRR. It also requires the submission of detailed state plans and annual performance reports and explicitly allows for the *discontinuance* of states that are not making significant progress in reducing the number of students reading below grade level.

Significant National Activities Funds—*Reading First* is allotted up to $25 million each year for National Activities. This allows the Department of Education to provide unprecedented funds for technical assistance and monitoring activities to support the implementation of *Reading First*. A specific, focused multi-million dollar contract has been awarded that will provide on-site monitoring in *each* state *each* year. Other well funded pending contracts will specifically support the competitive subgrant process across the nation and ongoing technical assistance for subgrantees.

Rigorous Application Process—The rigorous *Reading First* application process has not only sent the clear message to states that weak, substandard plans will not be funded, but it has also required each state to create a detailed blueprint of its *Reading First* plan. States have not been allowed to provide vague overviews of any facet of their plans. As a result, monitors will be able to assess whether states are implementing their plans exactly as approved.

Solid Relationships With State Education Agencies (SEAs)—The application process has provided an opportunity for relationship building between State program coordinators and federal *Reading First* program staff. Program staff is in frequent, ongoing contact with states in both the application and implementation phases.

Performance Reporting—States must submit an annual performance report documenting their progress in reducing the number of students reading below grade level. In their applications, states have had to describe how reporting requirements will be met. States will not be able to claim they do not have the appropriate data. States have also had to describe how they will make funding decisions, including discontinuation, based on the progress of participating districts and schools.

External Review—One important requirement of the *Reading First* program to enhance accountability is the implementation of an external independent review of the degree to which states and local school districts are increasing the number of students who read proficiently. The external review also evaluates whether all the essential components of reading assessment instruction are being implemented and taught consistently and with appropriate fidelity. The funding for this evaluation is sufficient to complete the review effectively. Results will be used to improve the implementation of *Reading First* and to insure that all students are learning to read.

Improving on REA—For all of these reasons, the implementation of *Reading First* will be stronger and more focused than preceding programs such as the *REA*. Unlike previous programs, *Reading First* provides an opportunity for students and teachers in classrooms in every state to participate, and all states will have the resources to use proven methods of reading instruction to improve student achievement. A major difference between *Reading First* and the *REA* is that all states and local districts are held accountable for ensuring that federal funds are explicitly tied to student reading achievement.

THE FEDERAL RESPONSE TO CONCERNS ABOUT LIMITATIONS IN EDUCATIONAL RESEARCH

Reyna has argued that the most important elements of the *NCLB* and the *ESRA* were not specific programs or policies, but the documented and explicit need to rely on the scientific method for generating and acquiring knowledge that will inform and guide instructional practices in the classroom. I agree and would add that the legislation also emphasized the need for transparency and accountability to assure the public that the instructional programs, strategies, and approaches provided to our children were indeed grounded in scientific evidence of effectiveness.

Not surprisingly, the federal requirement for evidence-based practices has led some in the educational research community to characterize both *NCLB* (including *Reading First*) and the *ESRA* as examples of government interference in the market place of research ideas and practices. Some argue that the *ESRA* legislation encourages only certain types of scientific inquiry (e.g., randomized controlled trials [RCTs]) and excludes researchers who conduct descriptive and qualitative research from opportunities for federal funding.   But this interpretation is wrong on at least two counts. First, as Reyna points out, the critical need for rigorous and trustworthy scientific evidence to guide and inform both educational policies and instructional practices was also underscored and recommended by leading members of the educational research community. Specifically, in its final report, the National Academy of Sciences Committee on Scientific Principles of Education Research (Shavelson & Towne, 2002) recommended increased rigor in education research and peer review and stressed the need for education research to adhere to the cannons of science as exemplified in other research fields addressing human development and learning. Second, the priority placed on the use of RCTs by the Institute of Educational Sciences (IES) to determine the effectiveness of educational programs and innovations clearly does not exclude quasi-experimental and single-subject designs when randomization is not feasible. The fact is however that the RCT is the methodological standard for what constitutes scientifically based evaluation methods for determining whether an instructional program or intervention is directly linked to improved outcomes.

The negative responses to the call for increased rigor in educational research may reflect more naivety than legitimate concern. A number of reviews of the quality of educational research have indicated that much of the research published in archival journals and disseminated to researchers, teachers, and policy makers is of uneven merit (Ellis & Fouts, 1997; Heath, 1999; Lagemann & Shulman, 1999). In the area of reading research alone, the National Reading Panel (NICHD, 2000) found that less than a third of published studies on the effectiveness of reading programs and interventions met basic scientific methodological criteria.

The reasons for the uneven quality of educational research are numerous, but it is possibly the case that some education researchers may have forgotten or were never taught that the trustworthiness of any research study is predicated on two major elements: (a) the suitability of the proposed research design and methodology to address the specific question(s) posed by the study; and (b) the scientific rigor of the methodology itself. The frequent mismatch between the research question and the appropriate methodology in education research is reflected in the persistent debates on the relative value of quantitative *or* qualitative research methods in identifying whether an instructional program is effective. Not only are these debates time consuming, they are irrelevant. The type of research method employed is solely a function of the questions under study. Qualitative, descriptive research cannot identify generalized instructional strategies that are directly linked to improvements in academic achievement—only well designed randomized controlled trials (or well-designed quasi experimental studies) can determine what works, what does not work, and what is harmful.

Obviously, studies that employ both types of design are important and frequently necessary if we are to develop the fullest and richest understanding of what specific instructional approaches are most effective for which children at which phase of development and under what particular conditions. But integrating research approaches in a thoughtful and appropriate manor demands a clear understanding among researchers of the assumptions underlying different research methods and the purposes for which the method is best suited. To be sure, over the past years, some educational research may have confused these assumptions and purposes to the detriment of children and teachers. The *NCLB and* the *ESRA* represent federal efforts to help reverse this trend.

SOME FINAL THOUGHTS

As Dr. Reyna explains, the scientific method and its application to the conduct of educational research is a wonderful example of democracy in action. She makes the critical point that scientific findings about what and how something works are continuously open to empirical challenges. If a particular finding overturns widely held philosophical beliefs or scientific findings about learning and teaching, that finding can also can be challenged objectively through replication and additional study. In this manner knowledge builds systematically and is honed through competing scientific challenges. Consider how much more productive this approach to knowledge generation is compared to the sometimes too frequent *ad hominem* abuse foisted on education scientists when their findings contradict well entrenched philosophical and ideological positions.

It is the case that building a high-quality education research infrastructure is only one step toward guiding instructional programs and practices through converging scientific evidence. There continues to be an alarming paucity of knowledge about how best to implement trustworthy research findings in complex environments such as schools and classrooms. We do not yet understand the incentive systems that will help teachers and school administrators better understand, respect and use scientific research to guide their instructional policies and practices. We also do not yet understand how to ensure that the educational researchers of tomorrow will become equipped to address the complexity of the research issues and questions not yet answered. The breadth and depth of their research training must be increased with similar opportunities provided for educational researchers now working in the field. I am convinced that the scientific standards demanded by *NCLB* and the *ESRA* will move the research community forward and am likewise convinced that the peer review process now in place within IES will help to establish the research quality that must be in place to ensure that no child is left behind.

REFERENCES

Adams, M. J., & Bruck, M. (1995a). Resolving the "great debate." *American Educator, 19,* 10–20.

Adams, M. J., & Bruck, M. (1995b). Word recognition: The interface of educational policies and scientific research. *Reading and Writing, 5,* 113–139.

Ellis, A. K., & Fouts, J. T. (1997). *Research on educational innovations* (2nd ed.). Larchmont, NY: Eye on Education.

Heath, J. (1999). Discipline and disciplines in education research: Elusive goals? In E. Lagemann & L. Shulman (Eds.), *Issues in education research: Problems and possibilities* (pp. 203–223). San Francisco: Jossey-Bass.

Kennedy, M. M. (1997). The connection between research and practice. *Educational Researcher, 26,* 4–12.

Lagemann, E. C., & Shulman, L. S. (Eds.). *Issues in education research.* San Francisco: Jossey-Bass.

Lyon, G. R. (2002). Reading development, reading difficulties, and reading instruction: Educational and public health issues. *Journal of School Psychology, 40,* 3–6.

Lyon, G. R., & Chhabra, V. (2004). The science of reading research and its importance to teaching reading. *Educational Leadership, 6,* 12-17.

Lyon, G. R., Shaywitz, S. E., Chhabra, V., & Sweet, R. (2004). Evidence-based reading policy in the United States: How scientific research informs instructional practices. In G. Reid & A. Fawcett (Eds.), *Dyslexia in context: Policy and practice* (pp. 130-146). London: Whurr.

Lyon, G. R., Fletcher, J. M., Shaywitz, S. E., Shaywitz, B. A., Torgesen, J. K., Wood, F. B., et al. (2001). Rethinking learning disabilities. In C. E. Finn, R. A. J. Rotherham & C. R. Hokanson (Eds.), *Rethinking special education for a new century* (pp. 259–287). Washington DC: Thomas B. Fordham Foundation and Progressive Policy Institute.

Lyon, G. R. (2002). Reading development, reading difficulties, and reading instruction: Educational and public health issues. *Journal of School Psychology, 40,* 3–6.

McDaniel, J. E., Sims, C. H., & Miskel, C. G. (2001). The national reading policy arena: Policy actors and perceived influence. *Educational Policy, 15,* 92–114.

McKenna, M. C., Stahl, S. A., & Reinking, D. (1994). A critical commentary on research, politics, and whole language. *Journal of Reading Behavior, 26,* 211–233.

Moats, L. C. (2000). *Whole language lives on: The illusion of "balanced" reading instruction.* http://www.ldonline.org/ld_indepth/reading/whole_language_lives_on.html; accessed November 25, 2003.

National Center for Educational Statistics. (2003). *National assessment of educational progress: The nation's report card.* Washington DC: U.S. Department of Education.

National Institute of Child Health and Human Development. (2000). *Report of the National Reading Panel. Teaching children to read: An evidence-based assessment of the scientific research literature on reading and its implications for reading instruction:*

Reports of the subgroups (NIH Publication No. 00-4754). Washington, DC: U.S. Government Printing Office.

President's Commission on Excellence in Special Education. (2002). *A new era: Revitalizing special education for children and their families.* Washington, DC: U.S. Department of Education.

Shavelson, R. J., & Towne, L. (2002). *Scientific research in education.* Washington, DC: National Academies Press.

Shaywitz, S. E. (2003). *Overcoming dyslexia.* New York: Knopf.

Stanovich, K. E. (2000). *Progress in understanding reading: Scientific foundations and new frontiers.* New York: Guilford Press.

Sweet, R. (in press). The big picture: Where are we nationally on the reading front? In P. McCardle & V. Chhabra (Eds.), *The voice of evidence in reading research.* Baltimore: Brookes.

Torgesen, J. K. (2002). Lessons learned from intervention research in reading: A way to go before we rest. In R. Stainthorpe (Ed.), *Literacy: Learning and teaching.* Monograph of the British Journal of Educational Psychology, London: British Psychological Association.

CHAPTER 7

RESPONSE TO REYNA'S THE *NO CHILD LEFT BEHIND ACT* AND SCIENTIFIC RESEARCH: A VIEW FROM WASHINGTON, DC

Douglas E. Mitchell

A political bandwagon carrying the banner of educational improvement through "scientific research" is rolling across the land accompanied by a groundswell of public interest and political pressure. Those managing it are promising dramatic changes in the definition of acceptable professional practice within the nation's schools. The result is a level of public, political and professional attention not seen since the outbursts accompanying release of the *Nation at Risk* report in 1983, or possibly the upsurge of national pressure for school reform following the 1957 launching of the Russian *Sputnik* space craft. Professor Reyna's detailed review of key provisions of the *No Child Left Behind Act* (NCLB) and the *Education Sciences Reform Act* (ESR) signed into law during 2002 documents the breadth and depth of congressional and presidential commitment to the new political

The No Child Left Behind *Legislation:*
Educational Research and Federal Funding, 89–96
Copyright © 2005 by Information Age Publishing
All rights of reproduction in any form reserved.

consensus. At its core is a call to shift control over standards for school programs and practices away from education professionals and into the hands of social and cognitive scientists. It is difficult, and possibly even dangerous to one's standing as a research scholar, to raise cautionary questions about what this sweeping change in national education policy might actually mean for the future of the nation's public schools, but my 3 decades as a student of educational policy and politics suggests that there are some important issues that need to be addressed if this bandwagon is not to become a political juggernaut, prone to crushing its most ardent admirers as well as those whose personal interests and political philosophies are leading them to resist its forward progress.

My cautionary concerns arise in four areas: (a) the technical idea of science that appears central to these policies, (b) the importance of grappling with questions of motivation and morality as well as those of technique when trying to build school improvement strategies, (c) the importance of considering how professional and scientific considerations can become integrated into the practice of teaching, particularly when the teacher workforce is drawn from the middle and lower ranks of the nation's college graduates, and (d) the importance of recognizing that schools are more aptly described as "social institutions" than as educational "service delivery organizations." Taken together, these concerns lead me to see the "science-based" bandwagon as in danger of producing tensions and stresses that are far less constructive than its enthusiasts are expecting.

SCIENCE IS MORE COGNITIVE THAN TECHNICAL

I begin with the idea of science ensconced in the landmark education reform legislation reviewed by Professor Reyna. Most interpretations of the scientific basis of school reform required by *NCLB* and *ESR*, including that presented by Professor Reyna, emphasize the technical more than the broader theoretical meanings of "science." The most common metaphor for the knowledge to be generated and used for school improvement is that of new drug development and other therapeutic techniques discovered by medical researchers. This view of science sees as its crowning achievements the mapping of cause and effect relationships within a well-established framework or paradigm of investigation. Certainly such research is vitally important to improvement of practice in all fields of human endeavor, including education. Studies of this type can be counted upon to generate substantial marginal improvements in any field where the core mechanisms of action are well conceptualized and ways of studying their operations adequately developed. Thus, in raising a cautionary question, I'm not in any way trying to negate the importance of this kind of work. I am quite concerned, however, that the current demand for science-based school program improvement is not giving nearly enough attention to the ways in which the most powerful scientific breakthroughs of the last 3 centuries have been more cognitive than technical. Even within the history of scientific medicine, the most important advances were the result of research work leading to dramatic reorganizations in thinking about disease, not just in the verification of the efficacy of specific treatments.

The idea of bacteria induced disease, for example, produced the radical reconceptualization needed to organize a search for antibiotic drugs. Later, the recognition that virus induced diseases differ fundamentally from bacterially induced ones spawned a very different search for new drugs and treatments. Still later, a focus on cancer and heart diseases once again reorganized the search for therapeutic interventions. And most recently, the conceptualization and mapping of the human genetic structure is creating a still different sort of research stream. There are some very important negative elements in this history as well. Misconceptions of health problems have led to dangerous and useless therapeutic technologies ranging from bloodletting and peach-pit cancer treatments to doubtful hormone therapies and dangerous drug administrations like the sad case of thalidomide or the recent recall of ephedra.

My point is simply that productive research requires more than reliable and valid techniques of data collection and analysis, it also requires a sound theoretical grasp of the underlying mechanisms at work in the domain of study and a broad enough definition of "proven techniques" to include a realistic appraisal of side effects as well as direct effects. Education is much weaker than medicine or physics in its grasp of basic mechanisms of action and I fear that we are facing the equivalent of insisting that virus diseases be treated with massive doses of antibiotics because we have proven that these antibiotics have been efficacious in treating some diseases.

LEARNING IS GROUNDED IN MOTIVATION AND MORALITY AS WELL AS TECHNIQUE

Concerns about the adequacy of the conception of science embedded in *NCLB* and *ESR* bring me to my second cautionary question. Teaching and learning involve important social, motivational and moral dimensions all too often ignored by the "science-based" reform advocates. When entrusting their children to the public schools, parents expect that family values and traditions will be both honored in daily practice and passed on to the next generation. While this trust is often breached, by cultural misalignment between families and professional educators, or by lack of skill or acceptance of family cultures on the part of school personnel, the history of education in this country is rife with social and political controversies surrounding these culture clashes. Indeed, from religious tolerance to racial integration these controversies have spilled over into violence or near violence and repeatedly reached the Supreme Court for adjudication.

The most pernicious and difficult to manage consequence of these culture clashes is the tendency for large numbers of students and their families to lose the motivation to participate or succeed. Where "science-based" is taken to mean using proven techniques to enhance instruction, the attack on this problem is often reduced to blaming educators for incompetence and asserting with increasing volume the shibboleth that "every child can learn." The result is to suppress awareness of the issues surrounding motivation and to redouble demands for technically "right practice."

The problem of motivation is, by no means, confined to students and their families. We are also facing severe problems of motivation on the part of professional educators. Attracting and retaining a sufficient number of qualified and energized teachers to staff the public schools is proving very difficult. And motivating them to understand and utilize innovative instructional techniques is also proving more difficult than many expect. More than half a century ago, however, social researchers started to learn a good deal about the problems of value conflict and performance motivation in a number of different occupational settings. Rural sociologists learned the profound truths about human motivation that lie behind the, probably apocryphal, story of the farmer who reportedly said, "I don't farm half so good as I could now, what do I need with your new seeds?" Innovative practices require more than technically adequate innovations to become incorporated into daily operations. These rural sociology studies have been repeated in numerous other occupational contexts. Both staff and students must be brought into the process in ways that enable them to believe that innovative techniques are meant to benefit rather than manipulate them. Linda McNeil (2000) documents the dramatic negative consequences for teachers resulting from imposition of the Texas standards-based educational reform—negative consequences that arose from problems of staff understanding and motivation, not problems of the technical adequacy of the imposed new techniques.

Once again, my point is simple, but its implications are profound. As David Cohen (1990) shows in his fascinating tale of "Mrs. Oublier's" abortive attempt to incorporate California's new math curriculum into her daily practice, innovative techniques are easily and often thoroughly corrupted when pressed upon a staff that does not fully understand them or are not adequately trained to utilize them properly. The result can actually make the "improved" educational process less productive of learning than would be produced by using less sophisticated techniques in more appropriate ways.

LINKING SCIENTIFIC AND PROFESSIONAL KNOWLEDGE IS NO SIMPLE MATTER

Professional practice involves finding strategies for effective action in complex contexts. By contrast, scientific research involves bracketing off the messy and hard to understand contextual variables (through randomization of treatments in controlled experiments) in order to identify the cause and effect relationships among critical variables. As a result, scientific findings are always, in principle, *ceteris paribus* (other things being equal) conclusions. In professional work, other things are *not* equal. Thus, the essence of good professional practice is to discern which "other things" can be safely disregarded and which cannot. While scientists can control "other things" through experimental controls and randomization of treatments, professionals control their work through the establishment of "standards of professional practice," which are drawn from the history of attempted interventions that have "done no harm" or at least had benefits that demonstrably outweighed their negative outcomes.

My point here is that science and professionalism represent very different ways of simplifying complex contexts in order to operate effectively within them. The simplification strategies are so different because the purposes of action are very different. The scientist wants to simplify in order to understand and interpret while the professional simplifies in order to take action, action in which those affected by the action are at risk of being damaged if actions are inappropriate. Certainly professional standards should include all of the scientific findings that have proven reliable and valid—*within the context of action in which the professional is currently working.* In most professional fields, however, there is also a lot of knowledge that has, like the secrets of gourmet cookery, been vouchsafed by outcome effects—effects that include consumer taste and satisfaction rather more than scientifically grounded nutritional benefits. Surely, educators should be shaken in their confidence that current educational practices are intrinsically superior to scientifically guided innovations, but they should not be dissuaded from relying upon accepted professional standards in areas where science offers oversimplification or no guidance at all. In short, science can support but it cannot replace professionalism in any human service activity where goals are diverse, motivations problematic or mechanisms of effective action not fully understood. The "science-based" reformers too often sound like they wish to dominate and direct rather than inform and support professional educators.

SCHOOLS ARE INSTITUTIONS, NOT ORGANIZATIONS

My final cautionary question about the "science-based" bandwagon has to do with the nature of the schools within which students and educators enact teaching and learning activities. Ever since publication of Raymond Callahan's classic, *Education and the Cult of Efficiency* (1962) we have realized that school systems are highly vulnerable to penetration by political and social forces seeking to redirect their programs and reconstruct their norms. These penetrations come from business organizations, religious groups, civil rights activists, political partisans of all stripes, labor organizations and a variety of other special and public interest pressure groups. More recently, beginning with the landmark study by Meyer and Rowan (1977), we have been able to describe in a convincing way the origins and the consequences of that vulnerability. The key to understanding this phenomenon lies in recognizing the crucial distinction between *organizations* and *institutions*. When, at the beginning of the 20th century, Max Weber declared bureaucracies to be the archetype of modern social organizations (and the modern period's crowning organizational achievement), he saw bureaucratic organizations as ones that place a high premium on rationality of action and of policy. Pragmatic and productivity goals are, in this ideal-type social organization, the fundamental *raison d'etre* of the organization and action. The establishment of bureaucratic goals was seen as the exclusive prerogative of senior executives, and it was assumed that members of the organization had agreed to pursue executive management's goals as part of the "social contract" making them members of the organization. As serious organizational research was undertaken during the middle half of the 20th century, however, it became clear that this ideal-typical conception of bureaucratic social organization does not adequately account much of what happens in complex social organizations. In particular, as noted by Meyer and Rowan, and elaborated by Powell and Dimaggio (1991), Meyer and Scott (1994) and Scott (2001), many complex organizations (especially schools) engage in a broad array of activities that are designed to garner legitimacy in the eyes of important environmental groups rather than pursue in any direct way the rational goals of the organization. These legitimacy-garnering activities, as the institutional theorists have documented, are not merely window-dressing activities that could be abandoned without consequence—they are absolutely essential to organizational health and survival.

It is probably not accidental that the advocates of "science-based" educational reform have specified as the consequence of failure to follow the dictates of this model of school improvement that public schools should be reorganized to more closely resemble small-scale private productive organizations. It is these organizations that most closely represent the Weberian ideal-type bureaucratic organizations and are most able to ignore institutional legitimacy considerations in their organizational form and action norms. But these small-scale bureaucracies are anachronistic in a globalized economy and in our integrated polyglot society. Small scale bureaucracies are great for the pursuit of diverse, privatized goals, but they cannot be expected to meet common standards or to be held accountable for meeting either equity or efficiency goals. It is intriguing that just as "bureaucracy" has become a synonym for unresponsive and irresponsible social organization, the most common proposal for what to do with "failed" schools is to turn them into small scale bureaucracies whose market survival is expected to guarantee that they are efficiently responsive to public and private pressures to increase performance. One needs only to look at the residential real estate market in this country to see an example of an industry run substantially by small scale private bureaucracies that, left to their own devices, succeeded in becoming one of the most persistent and pernicious blockages to equal housing opportunities.

Once again, my point is simple—schools exist as the institutional battlegrounds for cultural, ethnic and social class conflicts every bit as much as they represent production organizations designed to facilitate student learning. It is impossible to keep these value conflicts isolated and separated from instructional support systems. Thus, "science-based" must include the political, social and anthropological sciences as well as the psychological sciences that have had the most influence on *NCLB* and *ESR* conceptions of what sorts of research are likely to facilitate school improvement.

In sum, my concerns about *NCLB* and *ESR* do not arise from any resistance to the importance of social science research, but from an inescapable feeling that this round of high-profile politically driven school reform, like so many before it, suffers from narrowness of vision, overblown expectations, and a basic disrespect for the nature and complexity of the public schools. Just as the nation's health care problems are only partly scientific in character, so are its educational problems. There is, I am afraid, no chance whatsoever that education professionals will be given the lengthy training and socialization into practice that have been found to be essential in the fields of medicine, law, or architecture. Nor does this latest round of reforms promise any serious movement toward the kind of closely coordinated and supervised work essential to high quality engineering and business management. We are, in short, undergoing another round of highly intrusive, melodramatic school reform efforts where externally mandated practices are accompanied by threats to dismantle the public school system if educators do not make them work. By all means bring on the researchers, but try to remember that research findings can be properly utilized only if rank and file educators understand what they mean, are persuaded that they can be adapted to a complex and value-conflicted social environment, and will not undercut the motivation of students and staff in the process.

REFERENCES

Callahan, R. E. (1962). *Education and the cult of efficiency: A study of the social forces that have shaped the administration of the public schools.* Chicago, IL: University of Chicago Press.

Cohen, D. K. (1990). A revolution in one classroom: The case of Mrs. Oublier. *Educational Evaluation and Policy Analysis, 12,* 327–345.

McNeil, L. (2000). *Contradictions of school reform: Educational costs of standardized testing.* New York: Routledge.

Powell, W. W., & DiMaggio, P. J. (Eds.). (1991). *The new institutionalism in organizational analysis.* Chicago: University of Chicago Press.

Meyer, J., & Rowan, B. (1977). Institutionalized organizations: Formal structure as myth and ceremony. *American Journal of Sociology, 83,* 340–363.

Scott, W. R. (2001). *Institutions and organizations.* Thousand Oaks, CA: Sage.

Scott, W. R., & Meyer, J. W. (1994). *Institutional environments and organizations: Structural complexity and individualism.* Thousand Oaks, CA: Sage.

CHAPTER 8

THE *NO CHILD LEFT BEHIND ACT*

What if it Worked?

Angela M. O'Donnell

According to Reyna (this issue), the underlying assumptions that motivated the *No Child Left Behind* legislation included beliefs that current levels of academic achievement are too low, that there are grave consequences for the American economy if this situation persist, and the disparities in achievement across racial, ethnic, and socioeconomic groups are unacceptable. What if it worked? We would have a science of education that provided teachers, administrators with evidence-based instructional practices that would increase student achievement? An important question is whether we currently have sufficient knowledge or resources to hold schools accountable in the ways described in the legislation. Who could argue about the desirability of having all students succeed academically? Who could argue that society would not benefit from having a well educated citizenry or that all members of society, irrespective of race, ethnicity, or socioeconomic status are entitled to a quality

The No Child Left Behind *Legislation:*
Educational Research and Federal Funding, 97–102
Copyright © 2005 by Information Age Publishing
All rights of reproduction in any form reserved.

education? Perhaps because these outcomes are so desirable, the *No Child Left Behind Act* received broad support.

A key strategy in accomplishing these goals of having all students succeed in school is to use instructional practices and curricula that have been shown to be effective through scientific research. Concerns about the quality of educational research predate the passing of the legislation in the *No Child Left Behind Act* (2002) and the *Education Sciences Reform Act* (2002) and were shared by both educational researchers and governmental agencies. As early as 1995, the National Academy of Education established a commission to provide guidelines that would assist in making judgments about the quality of research. Other groups (FINE Foundation: Ducharme, Licklider, Matthes, & Vannatta, 1995; U.S. Department of Education's National Center for Education Statistics, NCES, 1991; National Science Foundation's Division of Research, Evaluation, and Communication, Suter, 1999) also worked to identify standards for the quality of educational research. In 1999, Kent McGuire, the assistant secretary of the Office of Educational Research and Improvement, alerted prospective grant writers to the importance of considerations of research quality and noted the continued debate about relevance and rigor of educational research.

Levin and O'Donnell (1999) noted the concerns expressed by various prominent educational researchers about the nature and quality of educational research and pointed out the need to improve the credibility of such research. They proposed to do so by recognizing that different research stages exist with different purposes, research questions, methodologies and standards of evidence, that the credibility of research will be enhanced by high standards of internal validity, that the creditability of research will be enhanced with high standards of external validity and importance, and finally, that randomized trials might be conducted. Levin and O'Donnell noted the importance of preliminary research (both laboratory-based and classroom-based research) in developing an understanding of the phenomena influencing classroom practice. However, further efforts beyond preliminary research are needed to determine if there are generalized practices that will work in a variety of contexts. Product development research in industry sets parameters on the fidelity of the product, defined as a tolerance of variability of performance of the product that is acceptable. We do not have that kind of knowledge about the variability in effects of instructional programs that are a result of different contexts. It is possible that we would discover that acceptable levels of effects of particular programs, instructional strategies, or curricula were not attainable in certain contexts. The National Academy of Science's Committee on Scientific Principles for Education Research (Shavelson & Towne, 2002) concluded that educational research is subject to the same scientific methods as other field. Like Levin & O'Donnell (1999), they suggested that the methods should fit the questions posed in the research. Increasing the quality of educational increase can only be a positive contributor to educational efforts.

The focus on scientific research is a key component of the *No Child Left Behind* legislation. This emphasis seems consistent with concerns already expressed by educational researchers. Reyna (this issue) notes that the four pillars the *No Child Left Behind Act* that will facilitate the accomplishment of these goals are "accountability for results, tempered by flexibility and local control, increases in choices available to parents of students attending Title 1 schools that fail to meet State Standards, and an emphasis on educational programs and practices that have been clearly demonstrated to be effective through rigorous scientific research." Educational research has always been significantly under-funded and the available database of scientific research related to educational issues is constrained by decades of underfunding. There is a certain circularity to requiring Title 1 assistance programs to use instructional strategies grounded in scientific research when the availability of such research is somewhat sporadic. There seems to be little analysis of whether there is a sufficient knowledge base of instructional strategies, curricular efforts, and professional development activities that have been *proven* effective to warrant the kinds of accountability that is described. There are clearly pockets of excellent research that would meet the standards of scientific research as set forth in the *No Child Left Behind* legislation (e.g., research on beginning reading). Can states actually draw on sufficient scientific research to provide the kinds of interventions mandated in schools that do not meet the standards set forth? If they cannot, what are the likely effects of the interventions they will provide?

A second key element of the new legislation is the notion of "accountability." The idea of holding schools accountable for the performance of its students has appeal. The requirement that a teacher be "qualified" is also appealing. The basic logic is that schools should use scientifically based practices to produce achievement results that meet state targets, and if they do not, there would be consequences for a school. The implication is that a parent should be able to send his/her child to an adequately performing school with qualified teachers. Viadero (2003) reported that studies conducted at Arizona State University suggest that high stakes testing produces few tangible academic gains. Under the new legislation, consequences that may accrue to schools that do not meet state targets include informing parents that the school is underperforming or the teachers are unqualified and the state and school are expected to take corrective action. A number of issues arise in considering these policies. As an example of the problems that arise, *Education Week* reported the problems experienced by a school in Pennsylvania. The school had received National Blue Ribbon honors in the three years prior to the 2003 academic year but was placed on a warning list in mid-August 2003 for failing to meet the state's standards for improvement (Gewertz, 2003). Upon appeal and with the availability of more recent data, the school was removed from the list. What is the effect on parents of school children in this school when they find out that their school received national recognition in the previous three years to suddenly find their school is on a warning list from the state? To which of these judgments (the school is on a state warning list, the school has national recognition) should they pay attention? Reyna (this issue) describes the imperfections of the legislation as being "mostly issues of implementation rather than principle." These problems of implementation are significant and have important effects on the morale of school personnel. In an era when there are large numbers of uncertified teachers in schools (particularly in urban areas), amplifying a punitive atmosphere in schools does not seem to be an effective strategy.

Reyna's (this issue) paper addresses the implications of the new legislation for the preparation of educational professionals. She identifies knowledge of cognition, research methodology, assessment, and statistics as knowledge that is necessary for educational professionals. She notes that topics in basic and higher order cognition are a must and asserts (without citation to research evidence) that "those who lacked this crucial knowledge would not be adequately prepared to make decisions about instructional approaches, textbook adoption, or other policies and practices intended to produce learning." Assuming this were true, it is not entirely clear which educational professionals will be making decisions about instructional issues.

Some states do not permit students to major in education at the college level. Implicit in this prohibition is the idea that there is insufficient content to warrant a major in the area. It is not surprising that the preparation of educational professionals against such a backdrop does not include rigorous training in research, assessment, or cognition. It takes more than a single course in research to be prepared to effectively reason about complex issues related to scientifically proven practices. Arguments about the importance of teachers' subject matter knowledge are often treated as arguments against the necessity for domain-general knowledge of pedagogy, human development, and cognition that Reyna argues for in this paper. Content knowledge alone does not make an effective teacher but is rather a necessary but insufficient condition to being one. If legislators and university administrators want to emphasize the scientific knowledge base necessary to preparing educational professionals, the depth and importance of that knowledge should be reflected in requirements for becoming such a professional.

Reyna (this issue) notes that there are a number of obstacles to educators accepting scientific evidence as the basis for settling disputes and laments the lack of critical thinking applied to educational claims. I would agree that the level of argumentation (from educational researchers, politicians, and the general public) needs to be elevated and more informed by data than by rhetoric. A low level of argumentation related to education has been present in many layers of society and is not helpful to creating a respect for educational professionals, without which progress is unlikely.

A new emphasis on educational science and a respect for it will assist in this endeavor.

What if this legislation worked? What if there was a substantive knowledge base of scientifically proven effective instructional practices that were identified? What if there was a "qualified" teacher in every classroom? Would we expect that the very disparities that motivated this legislation (e.g., insufficient levels of academic achievement, racial, ethnic, and socioeconomic differences in academic achievement) would disappear? Would we expect that the implementation of the provisions of this legislation would wipe out the effects of other influences on children's performance and academic achievement? In general, children spend only a portion of the year (approximately half) in school and only about a third of each day. Other forces besides schools and teachers influence children's beliefs about the role of schooling in their lives. Efforts to improve educational opportunity and accomplishment will need to go beyond classroom walls. A more scientific approach to education is long overdue. However, the humanistic nature of the enterprise should not be forgotten.

REFERENCES

Ducharme, M. K., Licklider, B. L, Matthes, W. A., Vannata, R. A. (1995). *Conceptual and analysis criteria: A process for identifying quality educational research*. Des Moines, IA: FINE Foundation.

Gewertz, C. (2003, October 8). PA adapts to new federal education law. *Education Week on the Web*. Retrieved Novermber 15, 2003, from http://www.edweek.org

Levin, J. R., & O'Donnell, A. M. (1999). What to do about educational research's credibility gaps? *Issues in Education, 5*, 177–229.

National Council for Educational Statistics. (1991). *SEDCAR (Standards for educational data collection and reporting)*. Washington, DC: U.S. Department of Education.

Shavelson, R. J., & Towne, L. (Eds.). (2002). *Scientific research in education*. Washington, DC: National Academy Press.

Suter, L. (1999, April). *Research methods in mathematics and science research: A report of a workshop*. Paper presented at the Annual Meeting of the American Educational Research Association, Montreal, Canada.

Viadero, D. (2003, January 8). Reports find faults with high-stakes testing. *Education Week on the Web*. Retrieved November 25, 2003, from http://www.edweek.org.

CHAPTER 9

EDUCATIONAL SCIENCE

More Than Research Design

Gary D. Phye

Being heavily involved with the evaluation of statewide entitlement grants that are impacted by the *No Child Left Behind Act* and the *Educational Sciences Reform Act,* my view from Iowa is consistent with that from Washington, DC, provided by Professor Reyna. In my opinion, she has provided an excellent synopsis of two of the most important federal education mandates enacted in the last 25 years, and they are directly impacting the practice of educational research today. This emphasis on the development of an educational science based on credible evidence is an opportunity for educational psychology as a discipline to again demonstrate its central position as a leader in this scientific endeavor. My point in the following dialogue is to emphasize that credible data, scientifically collected, must also follow from valid theory, metaphors and models. It must be reemphasized that when studying human behavior, credible data are a necessary but not sufficient condition for the development and implementation of models that describe, predict, and explain the human behavior under investigation.

The No Child Left Behind *Legislation:*
Educational Research and Federal Funding, 103–111
Copyright © 2005 by Information Age Publishing
All rights of reproduction in any form reserved.

As educational researchers have known for quite some time, three primary elements exist in any classroom setting and these are the learner, the teacher, and the environment. Obviously two of these elements involve the investigation of human behavior. Who better than educational psychology to bring psychological theory and research findings to the investigation of these elements? Each element contains variables (factors) contributing to the educational outcomes; at the same time, interactions among these elements are further sources of influence. Consequently, educational psychologists tend to concentrate research efforts on one of the primary elements (learner, teacher, and classroom environment). A point made 36 years ago by Edwards and Scannell (1968) is that:

> for educational psychology to be helpful to the teacher, human traits, and the environmental factors affecting human behavior must be defined and objectively measured. The findings of research may then be communicated. Improvement of professional education rests, in large part, on the ability of teachers to apply to concrete situations what psychologists have discovered about human behavior—particularly the learning process. (Edwards & Scannell, 1968, p. 2)

I read Professor Reyna's comments as a reaffirmation of what has traditionally been the central view of who educational psychologists are and what they do. I agree with Professor Reyna, that these initiatives will impact not only graduate programs and the way we currently train educational researchers, but they will also impact current research practices in education and educational psychology. Generally speaking, my comments are directed to educational researchers studying academic learning and achievement. More specifically, I am suggesting that educational psychology as a discipline re-examine its own status at this point in our long and illustrious history of scientific research—a history that can be traced back to the turn of the 20th century with the work of John Dewey, Edward L. Thorndike, and Charles H. Judd, among others. As experimental psychology at the beginning of the 20th century was moving away from a philosophical level of analysis and establishing itself as a discipline, two distinctive attributes of psychology can be noted. The pragmatism of William James (1890) set the functional tone for psychology that has been maintained through the twentieth century and into the twenty-first century. Generally speaking, functionalism is the view that mental processes and behaviors of living organisms help them adapt to their environments. This school of thought also flourished at the University of Chicago through the works of Dewey, Angell, and Carr. It should not be overlooked that the eminent sociologist George H. Mead was also at Chicago during this time. As has been pointed out by Bredo (1997), the historical roots of mainstream social constructivism in educational psychology can be traced back to the Chicago school and their approach to psychological functionalism.

In my following comments, I start with the basic premise that the *View from Washington, DC* is valid. My focus is on extending Professor Reyna's comments to encompass "method of science" issues that reflect current *philosophy of social science issues* that are critical considerations when the credible evidence being collected, analyzed, and interpreted is a measure of human behavior that we identify as academic learning or academic achievement. After all, educational research is a part of the social sciences enterprise.

The following comments are essentially an attempt to make three points. First, *experimentation* is the bedrock upon which credible data are collected. As a reminder, much of the learning research at the turn of the 20th century was being conducted in educational settings and involved methodological issues related to transfer (Judd, 1908; Thorndike & Woodworth, 1901a, 1901b,) and the need for the use of an independent control (Coover & Angell, 1907). These early research efforts to empirically address pedagogical questions helped established the experimental research tradition employed today by both experimental psychologists and educational psychologists. Ironically today, the hue and cry in some circles about the current emphasis on the use of comparison groups and random assignment in the development of credible educational research data has lead some educators to believe that this is a new and unreasonable practice.

Second, research design and credible data must also be evaluated from a *level of analysis* perspective. Level of analysis is a logical exercise that pertains to discipline, theory, metaphor, and model validation. For example, while philosophy has traditionally addressed issues involving the "nature of the human condition," psychology evolved as a discipline that sought to address issues of "human behavior." This distinction between human nature and human behavior should not be ignored. Historically, psychology as a discipline was predicated on the need to empirically observe behavior, and in a controlled manner attempt to explain the *functional relationship* of the observed behaviors. This second point pertains to the fact that the explanation sought was "causal" in nature (how do children learn? does this mode of instruction influence problem solving? etc.). Arguably, it is this seeking of causal explanations for human behavior that provides the functionalist tradition that characterizes psychology today.

The third point is that *adaptiveness* of behavior (functionalism) has been a central thesis of psychological inquiry, especially from Thorndike on, and the topic of learning has been a focus of theoretical development (Gibson, 1994). This emphasis on adaptiveness inevitably involves the investigation of such human characteristics as achievement motivation, self-efficacy, self-direction, individual differences in learning abilities, and so on. Consequently, the metaphor employed by educational researchers that should provide a story line or logically valid alignment from discipline, to theory, to model, to data interpretation is critical to our understanding of the data collected.

THE EXPERIMENTAL STUDY OF ACADEMIC LEARNING

Learning has so many meanings that it is necessary to first add a qualifying adjective. For example, in the applied setting we call the classroom, there are different types of learning experiences. Some experiences involve motor learning that serves as the basis for motor skill development. In some cases, learning activities focus on behavior that serves as the basis for social skills development. On the other hand, academic learning involves the processing and communication of cognitive information about the subject matter we teach in the classroom.

Having identified academic learning in terms of a "type of learning activity," scrutiny of a commonly accepted definition of learning serves as a means of considering what is frequently referred to as the "learning process." In the 3rd edition of *Learning Theories: An Educational Perspective*, Dale Schunk offers this suggestion. "*Learning* is an enduring change in behavior, or in the capacity to behave in a given fashion, which results from practice or other forms of experience" (Shuell, 1986; as cited in Schunk, 2000, p. 2). This definition of learning is consistent with a cognitive focus and captures the criteria most educational professionals consider central to learning.

EXPERIMENTATION

Three elements of Shuell's definition of academic learning (behavioral change, endurance, and practice) deserve further attention, because these elements help define the *level of analysis (experimental model)* involved in the present use of the term. Together these three elements stress the idea that academic learning is not typically a one-shot instructional experience. It is a process of: (a) acquiring new information, (b) the refinement and organization of what is already known, and (c) the successful use of that knowledge. Academic learning is the product of practice that provides the basis for relatively long-term change in one's personal knowledge. Ideally, this change will increase students' ability to be successful as they move from grade to grade where the curriculum requires more complex and specialized forms of personal knowledge.

From a research design perspective, our working definition of the academic learning process suggests three rather different paradigms for learning research. In each of these research paradigms, the dependent variable would be some measure of student performance in a subject matter area. An *acquisition learning paradigm* would be designed to assess change that occurs in student behavior or the capacity for that behavior (the dependent variable) over a period of active involvement. A *memory retention paradigm* would be designed to assess students' ability to remember under various conditions what had been learned during acquisition learning. Here, the interval between *acquisition learning* and *memory retention* may be immediate, hours, days, weeks, months, or years. Assuming that we have evidence of student remembering (memory retention), the next issue is to determine if the student can use this prior knowledge in order to generate new knowledge. Richard Mayer and Merlin Wittrock (1996) have suggested a *problem-solving transfer paradigm* as a means of investigating students' abilities to use prior knowledge to generate new knowledge.

Experimentation can be summed up using a minimalist definition as a process that involves some form of (a) empirical observation, (b) manipulation of the environment, and (c) efforts to control extraneous influences that might limit or bias observations. As such this definition lacks precision in terms of communication to fellow researchers about the nature of the observation (other than the fact that it is empirical), what was manipulated, or the nature of the control imposed. Consequently, in order to enhance not only communication among researchers but to also facilitate verification efforts via replication and the "scaling up" of scientifically based research findings, *operational definitions* are employed in all three elements of the aforementioned process of experimentation.

From an experimental perspective, operational definitions are the basis for both the enhancement of communication among researchers and the basis for promoting experimental replication and dissemination of "best practices." For example, if a research question concerns the impact of an educational intervention on student learning, one must design the study such that the consumer of this research can identify what is meant by *change* (e.g., test score improvement), *permanence* (e.g., 1 week, 1 month, or 1 semester, etc.), and *application* (e.g., near or far transfer).

ADAPTIVENESS AS A LEARNER CHARACTERISTIC

Level of analysis as an epistemological tool is used in psychological inquiry and is employed by Dr. Reyna when suggesting that teachers must demonstrate an understanding of the learning process in terms of the following cognitive functions that have been identified and described in detail in the learning, memory, and cognition literature.

> Topics in basic (attention, memory, and perception) and higher-order (reasoning, problem solving, and decision making) cognition are a must and would include: attention; working memory; learning processes (learning and retention); storage in and retrieval from long-term memory, interference and inhibition; executive function and monitoring; metamemory or memory strategies; meaning extraction (literal and figurative) for words, sentences, and discourse; inference and critical thinking (semantic, logical, and pragmatic inferences, situation models, and other mental representations); similarity, categorization, and analogical reasoning; non-verbal reasoning (e.g. spatial, scientific, and quantitative reasoning); domain specific knowledge (e.g. biology, calculus, or American history) and conceptual development; and judgment and decision-making. (Reyna, this volume, p. 19)

This use of levels of analysis is frequently employed in cognitive science and has been well documented by Stanovich (2001). However, when using levels of analysis as an epistemological tool, it is critical to insist on the assumption that there need not be a "cause-effect" relationship inferred between or among levels of analysis. Rather, the assumption of a *correspondence relationship* is made (Gibson, 1994). Thus, qualitative differences (differences in kind) as well as quantitative differences (differences in degree) may exist between or among corresponding levels of analysis. This theoretical assumption that is basic to functionalism keeps theory building from taking the simplistic route of assuming cause-effect relationships between levels of analysis that leads to the charges of reductionism and a mechanical model of human behavior as espoused by radical behaviorism of the 1960s.

MODELS, METAPHORS AND THEORY DEVELOPMENT

In any research activity that is couched in theory, metaphors and models guide theory building as a scientific activity. A specific example comes from the area of psycholinguistics. Within the context of language development, a distinction is made between *competency models* (rhetoric) and *performance models* (psychology). Competency models can be logically developed at a philosophical level of analysis without direct observation or empirical testing. Performance models employ a psychological level of analysis, require direct observation, and frequently start with the assumption that individual differences in human behavior preclude the exclusive use of a competence model as an explanation for human behavior.

This distinction between theoretical models (competency or performance) must be maintained by educational researchers. Otherwise, confusion reigns when theoreticians attempting to address questions of pedagogy confound these two very different types of models. I contend that this is one of the primary reasons that the implementation of educational research (including much of educational psychology research) frequently fails when moved into the realm of pedagogical practices.

While a failure to distinguish between competency and performance models can confound theory development, the selection of appropriate metaphors is also important. A brief comment about the impact of metaphors on data interpretation follows and focuses on the "functional memory metaphor" (performance model) and the "computer metaphor" (competency model). Cognitive scientists tend to view the academic learning process from a common level of analysis (information processing). However, by ignoring the basic assumptions inherent to competency and performance models, an understanding of the learning process that informs instructional design becomes confounded.

FUNCTIONAL MEMORY METAPHOR

During the last part of the 1960s and the decade of the 1970s, the cognitive revolution (Neisser, 1967) in the theoretical study of human learning and proliferated as a result of new data collection instruments and advances in research practices. In experimental psychology, learning was approached as "learning, memory and cognition." The "functional memory" metaphor was guiding much of the research efforts in learning and the level of analysis was an information processing approach. The functional memory metaphor is an organic model and research efforts focus on the identification of functional cognitive components such as short-term memory, working memory, long-term memory storage and retrieval, implicit memory, explicit memory, consciousness, etc. In other words, the memory metaphor was a new theoretical approach to describing and explaining cognitive activities that support human learning.

COMPUTER METAPHOR

The computer metaphor has been an extremely valuable tool that has helped provide a context for theory development in terms of research questions addressed and has strongly influenced the way we currently study instructional design in educational settings. The computer metaphor also provides the basis for an information processing level of analysis of the academic learning process. This level of analysis has been very valuable in the development of research questions involving instructional or teaching issues and issues involving classroom settings.

However, an information processing level of analysis based on the computer metaphor has its shortcoming. For instance, as an inorganic model, the computer metaphor has little to offer in terms of either motivation issues or a consideration of individual differences. These learner characteristics are extremely important contributors to learning activities in the classroom. The computer metaphor has little to offer on either count. Even from an information processing point of view, the computer metaphor has limited our thinking about transfer and problem solving as learner characteristics. For example the computer metaphor contributes to a view of memory processing of prior knowledge as basically a "storage or warehouse" phenomenon. With the computer metaphor, there can be an over reliance on an input side–storage–automatic retrieval–explanation of cognitive processing when attempting to understand the academic learning process (Phye, 2001). In this respect, the restrictions placed on learner abilities or characteristics by using a mechanical model of information processing is reminiscent of the operant condition model of learning circa 1950/1960.

In summary, it is the human memory metaphor that puts the learner at the center of the research process when attempting to address academic learning issues involving adaptability in the classroom (transfer and problem solving performance). In contract, much of what we currently see in articles published by educational researchers are manipulations of instructional variables and comparisons of method A versus method B. This research is quite good as far as it goes. Unfortunately, unless we do a better job of putting the learner and the teacher (human beings trying to adapt to a classroom learning episode) back into the equation, our ability to describe, predict, and explain academic learning in terms of human abilities and characteristics are limited.

I suspect that this last issue of mixing metaphor may be a problem for educational researchers who traditionally approach the development of research questions from an eclectic point of view. Eclecticism itself is not a problem if the theoretical alignment of metaphors and models that drives research hypotheses is aligned with research designs and methods that clearly articulate rather than confound the development of scientifically based research studies. In other words, there are theoretical distinctions to be made in educational research between studies of classroom instruction and studies of academic learning. I am simply suggesting that the metaphor upon which the research design is based will dictate the research design and statistical analyses that follow. Practically speaking, this confounding will produce an "explanation of findings" (however credible from a design perspective) that make the successful implementation of scientifically based research difficult at best.

REFERENCES

Bredo, E. (1997). The social construction of learning. In G. D. Phye (Ed.), *Handbook of academic learning: Construction of knowledge* (pp. 3–45). San Diego: Academic Press.

Coover, J. E., & Angell, F. (1907). General practice effect of special exercise. *American Journal of Psychology, 18*, 328–340.

Edwards, A. J., & Scannell, D. P. (1968). *Educational psychology: The teaching-learning process.* Scranton, PA: International Textbook.

Gibson, E. J. (1994). Has psychology a future? *Psychological Science, 5*, 69–76.

James, W. (1890). *Principles of psychology.* New York: Holt Reinhart & Winston.

Judd, C. H. (1908). The relation of special training to general intelligence. *Educational Review, 36*, 28–42.

Mayer, R. E., & Wittrock, M. C. (1996). Problem-solving transfer. In D. C. Berliner & R. C. Calfee (Eds.), *Handbook of educational psychology* (pp. 47–62), New York: Macmillian.

Neisser, U. (1967). *Cognitive psychology.* New York: Appleton-Century-Crofts.

Phye, G. D. (2001). Problem-solving instruction and problem-solving transfer: The correspondence issue. *Journal of Educational Psychology, 93*, 571–578.

Reyna, V. (2005). The *No Child Left Behind Act* and scientific research: A view from Washington, DC. In J. S. Carlson & J. R. Levin (Eds.), *Scientifically-based education research and federal funding agencies: The case of the* No Child Left Behind *legislation* (Vol. 1, pp. 1-25). Greenwich, CT: Information Age.

Schunk, D. H. (2000). *Learning theories: An educational perspective* (3rd ed.). Upper Saddle River, NJ: Merrill.

Shuell, T. J. (1986). Cognitive conceptions of learning. *Review of Educational Research, 56*, 411–436.

Stanovich, K. E. (2001). The rationality of educating for wisdom. *Educational Psychologist, 36*, 247–251.

Thorndike, E. L., & Woodworth, R. S. (1901a). The influence of improvement in one mental function upon the efficiency of other functions: The estimation of magnitudes. *The Psychological Review, 8*, 384–395.

Thorndike, E. L., & Woodworth, R. S. (1901b). The influence of improvement in one mental function upon the efficiency of other functions: Functions involving attention, observation, and discrimination. *The Psychological Review, 8*, 553–564.

CHAPTER 10

WHAT ROLE SHOULD THE GOVERNMENT PLAY IN A SCIENCE OF EDUCATION?

Michael Pressley

I doubt that there is anyone anywhere more firmly committed to the proposition that the scientific study of learning and related fields should inform education. For the past 30 years, most of my professional effort has been spent generating research and writing that was intended to impact education. And, you know what? Educational researchers have had quite a bit of impact over those 3 decades. My generation of educational scientists has made a difference.

I spent this morning in a school doing some observational work connected with an ongoing study. I saw something happen there that would not have happened in school 30 years ago. A fifth-grade teacher conducted a lesson about generating mental images during reading in order to understand and remember stories being read. How can I be so certain that did not occur 30 years ago? Because 30 years ago, I did some of the pioneering research on teaching children to generate mental images when they read (e.g., Pressley, 1976; see Pressley, 1977, for a review of the field at that time). I can tell you for absolutely certain that teachers were

The No Child Left Behind *Legislation:*
Educational Research and Federal Funding, 113–120
Copyright © 2005 by Information Age Publishing
All rights of reproduction in any form reserved.

not providing lessons about mental imagery generation back in the early to middle 1970s, for I was in many, many schools in that era, with not a hint of such instruction except when my colleagues and I provided it to students in experimental conditions (e.g., see Levin, 1973). It was gratifying to watch that lesson this morning, just as it has been gratifying to watch schools now using fuller comprehension instructional packages that were developed and evaluated in the past quarter-century by educational scientists working with educators (e.g., Anderson, 1992; Brown, Pressley, Van Meter, & Schuder, 1996; Palincsar & Brown, 1984; Pressley, El-Dinary, et al., 1992), responding, in part, to Durkin's (1978–1979) call for more teaching of comprehension in the middle and late elementary grades.

In fact, if you spend time at all in American elementary schools, it will not be long before you encounter kindergarten students receiving lessons to stimulate phonemic awareness, beneficiaries of research in the 1980s that was first summarized prominently by Adams (1990). Also, there have been systematic phonics programs in schools for more than a century, with plenty more of them appearing in the past quarter century in the wake of Chall's (1967) analysis in favor of synthetic phonics over the whole word method used in Dick and Jane readers. Then, there is process-writing instruction, which occurs in many elementary classrooms every morning, resembling nothing that was offered as writing instruction in the 1970s and before. Hayes and Flowers (1980) research on writing as recursive planning, drafting, and revising spawned research that has dramatically changed the way American children are taught to write (National Writing Project & Negin, 2003), with especially excellent research now informing the teaching of elementary, middle school, and high-school students who are struggling writers (Graham & Harris, 2003). How about conceptual approaches to mathematics instruction, which are flourishing in the contemporary school place, an approach supported by research data (e.g., Connected Mathematics; see Ridgway, Zawojewski, Hoover, & Lambkin, 2003)? Indeed, the only way to conclude that educational research has not impacted educational practice is to ignore most of the data to the contrary, which seems to be Reyna's (this issue) approach.

I have read the research that supports the educational efforts I just cited, as well as much of the literature supporting evidence-based education. A whole instructional program is rarely studied or evaluated, nor is the evaluation ever conducted over a population of students representative of the country. Rather, research efforts focus on a small aspect of the program (e.g., at one grade level), with the test almost always involving convenience samples (e.g., students in school districts who do not now use a program but would like to try it). Given that awareness, I chuckle as I contemplate the possibility of evidence-based, comprehensive educational programs being subjected to fully randomized experimental trials that provide comprehensive information about who the program works for and when, which seems to be the envisionment of Reyna and others now in Washington.

I chuckle despite the fact that I think such work could be appealing to me as an educational scientist. If the work were done with sufficient measurement of instructional process and intermediate outcomes, rather than just focusing on summative standardized test scores, so favored by the current federal administration, we might learn quite a bit about instruction. Why do I chuckle then? By the time even a single study was designed, executed, analyzed, written up, and disseminated, the version of the program tested would be an historic relic. All published, instructional programs, such as comprehensive reading instructional programs, revise regularly to meet new state mandates. In addition, especially since the onset of the government's evidence-based emphasis, reading programs are revised to incorporate new scientific understandings. The pace of instructional program experimentation could never keep up with such evolving, state-of-the-science/art comprehensive curricular programs.

Need to be convinced? Do a thought experiment. Suppose the 2002 version of the Open Court program, which I co-authored (and, thus, know for certain the realities of its production and revision schedule), had been randomly assigned to school districts at the moment it came off the press in autumn 2001. Data on the first year of the program would have been generated in school year 2001–2002. With talented data analysts and researchers writing up that data, perhaps a good draft of the paper would have been available by summer 2003, submitted to a journal, and maybe accepted by summer 2004, published at the beginning of 2005. A new edition of Open Court will appear in autumn 2004, several months before the data would be published. But, the situation is even worse than it seems. Are we really interested only in the impact of the program for 1 year? No, real children can experience a comprehensive reading program for 2, 3, and sometimes as many as 8 years (i.e., pre-K through grade 6). If we waited for 3 years of data, the study would be available to the public in summer 2006, which coincides with the publication date of what will be yet another revision of Open Court. Of course, the situation gets worse with evaluations of 4, 5, or more years of experiencing a reading program. With respect to the comprehensive educational interventions that children actually experience, randomized field trials probably are not realistic because they take too long relative to the market lifespan of the programs.

That said, I suspect that we are going to see some experimental evaluations of comprehensive instructional programs that are informed by research. If you actually performed in your own head the thought experiment suggested above, you realize that such studies are going to be expensive. If we are successful at all in getting even one or a few such studies, we will be very fortunate. In fact, with respect to most important educational problems, there are usually only a few experimental evaluations, if there are any at all (Cook, 2002).

To read Reyna and other Washington insiders who think like her (e.g., see Lyon & Chhabra, 2004), you might believe that no educational decisions could be made on the basis of a single study, for a single study cannot provide information about the reliability of a finding. Those making this point often mutter something about multiple field-based, experimental trials and medical research as they sermonize about how education should be more scientific. As it turns out, sometimes physicians do make decisions on the basis of single experiments. I probably owe my life to such intelligent decision making.

In early 1998, I was diagnosed with Stage 3 adenocarcinoma of the esophagus. The conventional treatments available at the time had a poor track record. My doctor recommended a treatment that enjoyed support in one true experiment conducted in the British Isles (Walsh et al., 1996). I read the Walsh et al. article, as I reflected on the recommendation to undergo the experimental treatment, involving chemotherapy and radiation in advance of surgery to shrink the tumor. Although there was only this one experiment, there were correlational data that this new approach to treatment was having an impact in contrast to decidedly ineffective conventional treatments. But, there was one other critical piece of data that impacted me. The lead physician for my case, who had decades of experience in treating the disease I had, offered the following observation during a consultation with him: "Since we started shrinking the tumors before surgery, patients have been doing a lot better." I decided to undergo the innovative treatment, for I respected the doctor's thinking, which was informed by all of the data that were available and his own extensive clinical experience, including with both the experimental treatment and the conventional approaches. I was cured of cancer of the esophagus.

There has never been a randomized experiment in the United States on the treatment I endured, not because the government would not fund it, but because doctors would not recommend patients enroll in the clinical trial, apparently convinced, like my physician, that pre-operative shrinkage was the way to go (Enziger & Mayer, 2003). Moreover, despite subsequent experimental trials in other parts of the world that have not yielded outcomes supporting the treatment I endured, pre-operative shrinkage continues as a favored option in this country (Enziger & Mayer, 2003). Sometimes excellent physicians depend on something other than the box score of a series of randomized trials. Sometimes they rely on a single experiment supported by correlational data and their own professional experiences. As a scientist, I look at the track record on the treatment I endured and continue to believe it is the right approach: The odds of surviving cancer of the esophagus are terrible with the conventional treatment. As far as I can tell, there are no data suggesting the treatment I experienced ever decreases the chance of survival and some data that it increases the chance of survival. I am with the doctors electing the experimental treatment.

In my own professional life, I make recommendations based on only a very little bit of experimental evidence all the time. One of the most prominent is my recommendation that elementary teachers teach comprehension strategies using a transactional approach. There are only two really well controlled comparisons of transactional strategies instruction (Anderson, 1992; Brown et al., 1996) and one well-done experiment of an intervention similar enough that I count it as data in favor of transactional strategies instruction (Collins, 1991). In all three studies, the effects of comprehension strategies instruction were large and observed over a variety of measures, including the standardized tests so embraced by the current administration. Each of the three experiments was so expensive and took so long to design, execute, and analyze that I am certain there will never be many well-controlled experiments or quasi-experiments on the approach. But, the experimental literature includes lots of validation of each of the component strategies taught as part of transactional comprehension strategies packages and plenty of nonexperimental evidence that such instruction dramatically changes how students process what they read (Pressley, El-Dinary, et al., 1992). As a scientist deeply immersed in this problem for several decades, I feel very confident in my recommendation, not just because of the three well-controlled evaluations of transactional strategies instruction but because of the related data as well. Oh, and then, there is one more thing. Whenever I have been around schools and classrooms where they are doing transactional strategies instruction, the teachers are always convinced that reading is better. Moreover, I am impressed that the students experiencing transactional instruction seem to have more intelligent, interpretive insights about what they are reading than in other classrooms I visit, especially those that include no mention of comprehension strategies. My 3 decades of immersion in schools has provided me with personal knowledge of reading instruction that increases my confidence in the outcomes of the controlled evaluations of transactional strategies instruction.

Should we permit politicians to determine how instructional science is done? Reyna seems to think so. I do not agree. Although educational scientists need the financial support of the government to do our work, we do not need the government's technical assistance, which often is naïve to say the least. For example, if you read Reyna's remarks, you might think that the reports from government panels are scientific documents. They are not. Scientific documents are peer reviewed and not published until the peers approve. That is not the standard the government has for publishing analyses, for example, the National Reading Panel (2000) report—which falls well below the criteria that a peer-reviewed document claiming to survey the scientific literature related to reading instruction would have to meet to appear in a selective scientific outlet. The government should leave the science to the scientists and stop attempting to foist their political efforts on the public as the equivalent of science. Reyna's (this issue) article is about the contemporary politics of education and not a bit about an educational science that any well-informed and conscientious educational scientist should accept.

Does the government have a right to demand particular educational outcomes? In fact, I would go further and say the government is obliged to demand that schools educate children to the maximum of their potential. What those maximums are should be determined through educational research, however, rather than congressional debate. Again, the government's main responsibility here is to decide such work should be done and provide funds for such work, not dictate how that work should be conducted.

My reading of the many complaints of underfunding of educational research and education more generally is that the federal government is not living up to its obligations here. Look carefully at the many research and educational programs Reyna mentions in her article—and, I mean, by reading the legislation and noting especially the funds appropriated for the work. You will be shocked at what the government is expecting from each of these programs relative to what the government is willing to pay. Rather than attempting to provide technical advisement on educational research to the researcher community, I would urge the politicians to focus on increasing their own technical expertise in generating the funds required if the nation is to have an expansively informative educational science that permits development of evidence-based curriculum and instruction that schools can afford to implement. More unfunded mandates to the educational scientific community and educators will only result in more irritated responses to the politicians, such as this one. The government's job is to raise and allocate resources for what needs to be done, a responsibility that seems more failed than accomplished with respect to education generally and educational research, in particular.

So, do I have a concrete suggestion for increasing the amount of high-quality educational research that impacts practice? I do. Fund the individuals who have contributed work in the past that has made a difference to education that has resulted in evidence-based interventions. Also fund graduate students to train with these scholars. Then, leave the researchers with track records and their students alone to do their work and make their research contributions. At the same time, make start-up grants to researchers who have not yet contributed to evidence-based education, when they show a desire to turn their attentions in that direction. And, then, find a way to provide incentives to all of those doing educational research to work with the practitioner and educational materials development communities to translate their research findings into practices and products that will be adopted in schools because they make sense to educators who understand the needs of their students and the country. The future of the country very much depends on policy makers forging a constructive relationship with researchers and educators that results in a far better education than many children in America are now receiving. I do not think that the Bush administration policies that Reyna describes have the potential to inspire the constructive relationships that are needed if education is to become intelligently evidence-based.

REFERENCES

Adams, M. J. (1990). *Beginning to read*. Cambridge, MA: Harvard University Press.

Anderson, V. (1992). A teacher development project in transactional strategy instruction for teachers of severely reading-disabled adolescents. *Teaching & Teacher Education, 8*, 391–403.

Brown, R., Pressley, M., Van Meter, P., & Schuder, T. (1996). A quasi-experimental validation of transactional strategies instruction with low-achieving second grade readers. *Journal of Educational Psychology, 88*, 18–37.

Chall, J. S. (1967). *Learning to read: The great debate*. New York: McGraw-Hill.

Collins, C. (1991). Reading instruction that increases thinking abilities. *Journal of Reading, 34*, 510–516.

Cook, T. D. (2002). Randomized experiments in education: Why are they so rare? *Educational Evaluation and Policy Analysis, 24*, 175–199.

Durkin, D. (1978-79). What classroom observations reveal about reading comprehension instruction. *Reading Research Quarterly, 14*, 481–533.

Enzinger, P. C., & Mayer, R. J. (2003). Medical progress: Esophageal cancer. *New England Journal of Medicine, 349*, 2241–2252.

Graham, S., & Harris, K. R. (2003). Students with learning disabilities and the process of writing: A meta-analysis of SRSD studies. In H. L. Swanson, K. R. Harris, & S. Graham (Eds.), *Handbook of learning disabilities* (pp. 323–344). New York: Guilford.

Hayes, J., & Flower, L. (1980). Identifying the organization of writing processes. In L. Gregg & E. Steinberg (Eds.), *Cognitive processes in writing* (pp. 3–30). Hillsdale NJ: Erlbaum.

Levin, J. R. (1973). Inducing comprehension in poor readers: A test of a recent model. *Journal of Educational Psychology, 65*, 19–24.

Lyon, G. R., & Chhabra, V. (2004). The science of reading research. *Educational Leadership, 61,* 12–17.

National Reading Panel. (2000). *Teaching children to read: An evidence-based assessment of the scientific research literature on reading and its implications for reading instruction.* Washington, DC: National Institute of Child Health and Development.

National Writing Project & Nagin, C. (2003). *Because writing matters: Improving student writing in our schools.* San Francisco: Jossey-Bass.

Palincsar, A. S., & Brown, A. L. (1984). Reciprocal teaching of comprehension- fostering and monitoring activities. *Cognition and Instruction, 1,* 117–175.

Pressley, G. M. (1976). Mental imagery helps eight-year-olds remember what they read. *Journal of Educational Psychology, 68,* 355–359.

Pressley, M. (1977). Imagery and children's learning: Putting the picture indevelopmental perspective. *Review of Educational Research, 47,* 586–622.

Pressley, M., El-Dinary, P. B., Gaskins, I., Schuder, T., Bergman, J. L., Almasi, J., & Brown, R. (1992). Beyond direct explanation: Transactional instruction of reading comprehension strategies. *Elementary School Journal, 92,* 511–554.

Ridgway, J. J., Zawojewski, S., Hoover, M. V., & Lambdin, D. V. (2003). Student attainment in the Connected Mathematics curriculum. In S. Senk & D. R. Thompson (Eds.), *Standards-based school mathematics curricula: What are they? What do students learn?* Hillsdale, NJ: Erlbaum.

Walsh, T., Noonan, N., Hollywood, D., Kelly, A., Keeling, N., & Hennessy, T. P. J. (1996). A comparison of multimodal therapy and surgery for esophageal adenocarcinoma. *New England Journal of Medicine, 335,* 462–467.

CHAPTER 11

SCIENTIFIC RESEARCH IS PROGRAMMATIC

Daniel H. Robinson

To say that Reyna's article resonated with my views would be an understatement. Few educational researchers are more pleased than I am to see the pendulum finally swinging away from postmodernism/constructivism and back to addressing important issues using experimental methods. As one who has conducted several experiments using random assignment, I am definitely a member of the choir listening to Reyna's sermon. Over the past 15 years, I have witnessed firsthand the field of education, as represented by the AERA conference and several educational journals, de-emphasizing experimental research. A few years ago, I stopped collecting data for the most part, having reached maximum disgust of the entire review process.

My disgust has been reduced as of late by the recent *NCLB* legislation and the efforts of people like Russ Whitehurst and Valerie Reyna to return educational research to a respectable status. Although this effort has a considerable ways to go, it is encouraging that so many prominent educational researchers have banded together in an attempt to ensure that we do not slip back into the abyss of relativism. Educational research seems

The No Child Left Behind *Legislation:*
Educational Research and Federal Funding, 121–128
Copyright © 2005 by Information Age Publishing
All rights of reproduction in any form reserved.

once again to be in the business of helping kids learn to enable empowerment. Finding the best ways that this can be accomplished is what we are all about. Reyna (this issue) mentions that if the *NCLB* legislation is to succeed, changes must be made in the kind of educational research that is conducted and in how we prepare prospective educational researchers (p. 2). The purpose of my commentary is to offer suggestions as to how these changes might be accomplished.

As Reyna also noted, it has been psychology departments rather than colleges of education that have provided most of the scientific evidence over the past several years (p. 7). Whitehurst (2003) in his AERA address presented the findings of a study that examined three journals from 1993–2002, two published by AERA—the *American Educational Research Journal* (AERJ) and *Educational Evaluation and Policy Analysis* (EEPA), and one published by APA—the *Journal of Educational Psychology* (JEP). Whitehurst noted that the field of psychology (JEP) as compared to education (AERJ and EEPA) published far more experimental articles and far fewer qualitative articles. In an effort to examine these differences more closely, a team of graduate students here at the University of Texas and I recently completed a study of the types of research published in five empirical educational psychology journals from 1995–2002 (Chung et al., 2004). Among the trends were considerable declines in the percentage of articles that reported intervention research and those that used experimental methods. Even in the JEP, intervention articles that used experiments had declined from about 50 percent to about one-third. Another educational psychology journal, *Contemporary Educational Psychology,* dipped from 28 to 14 percent. Least surprising was AERJ, which declined from 17 to zero percent, completing its transformation to a nonexperimental journal. So, although Whitehurst painted a favorable picture for the JEP compared with education journals, the fact is that experimental research, the kind *NCLB* and the IES are saying we need more of, is becoming increasingly rare in education and educational psychology.

But why is experimental research becoming increasingly rare? Why the rise in descriptive and correlational research studies that do not permit evaluation of what works? Somehow, many educational researchers and potential researchers got the notion that conducting experiments was no longer important and/or needed. In the postmodern shark tank known as colleges of education during the 1990s, conducting experimental research was certainly not in vogue and even criticized. I realize that the following personal anecdotal evidence does not qualify as the kind of scientific evidence Reyna calls for, but in the absence of the latter, I present the former. I recall describing an idea for an experimental study as a graduate student at the University of Nebraska to my peers and being received with laughter and snickering about how this approach was obsolete. Several years later I was presenting some research during an interview at a midwestern university that touted its college of education as one that embraced a constructivist philosophy. During the talk, I was verbally attacked by the angry audience, asking what nerve I had in conducting experiments to answer research questions (Ron Carver was my lone defender).

Now the pendulum seems to have shifted and our silly obsession with postmodernism is subsiding. Nevertheless, I believe another movement that has emerged over the past 20 years, almost in parallel to postmodernism, has also discouraged people from conducting experimental research—the rise of meta-analysis. An absurd accusation, you say? Glass (1976), when first introducing meta-analysis, openly wondered whether well-designed and poorly designed experiments give very different findings. If this is true, how much effort should we put into designing and conducting experiments? Schmidt (1996), in his influential article 8 years ago, concluded: "Clearly, at this point the need is not for more primary research studies but for some means of making sense of the vast number of accumulated study findings. This is the purpose of meta-analysis" (p. 123) and "[t]oday, many discoveries and advances in cumulative knowledge are being made not by those who do primary research studies but by those who use meta-analyses" (p. 127). Thus, it seems as though meta-analysts feel that we have enough primary studies and conducting more experiments in unnecessary.

Meta-analysts, rather than collecting primary research data, collect studies as their data points. I refer to this type of educational research as armchair or office research, since the researcher is not required to ever enter a classroom or interact with students (I am not casting stones as I have done my share of this type of research). For most meta-analysts, the goal is to reach a conclusion about whether a previously touted or criticized effect is valid by pooling all the research on that effect and then averaging the effect sizes to see if they are positive or negative, minimal or considerable. Because there are a plethora of individual studies out there on just about anything, it is easy to see why some people would be led to believe that we no longer need to do more studies. If we can simply analyze the studies that have been conducted so far, perhaps we can shed new light on the overall findings.

This line of thinking has been influential in fueling the controversy concerning whether statistical significance testing has a place in research. For meta-analysts, whether single studies are significant is not a concern. Simply average the effect sizes and you will have an unbiased look at the effect. Thus, there has been an "effect size movement" (Robinson, Whittaker, Williams, & Beretvas, 2003) over the past 10 years or so where more and more journals are requiring authors to report effect sizes. As meta-analysts look at the wasteland of single-experiment studies out there, each dichotomously classifying their findings as significant or not, they rightfully become dismayed with significance testing (e.g., Cohen, 1990; 1994). Schmidt (1996) noted that "[a]s conclusions from research literature come more and more to be based on findings from meta-analysis, the significance test necessarily becomes less and less important" (p. 116).

The fact that educational research is characterized more by single, piecemeal studies rather than investigations that involve a series of studies may be the culprit. And where do educational researchers first learn that conducting and publishing single studies is the norm? Think of the first course in statistics. How are the research examples presented in introductory statistics textbooks? Because of space considerations/limitations, small sample studies are described and students are encouraged to interpret the outcome of such single-shot studies as either significant or not. Eventually, students move on to the dissertation proposal. The dissertation is supposed to be a "study." It is a grandiose study, one that will not only impress the committee but also get the student national recognition, and hopefully a job. Thus, students begin to think in graduate school that to make it in this profession is to design successful studies.

Glass (2000) suggested that educational research would do well to move away from the notion that research is simply doing studies and instead think of contributing in terms of dosage-response curves. I believe this will be best accomplished if educational researchers stop publishing single-shot studies and instead begin publishing multiple experiments that are programmatic in nature. This idea is certainly not new and has been promoted emphatically by Joel Levin when he served as editor of the *Journal of Educational Psychology*. The need for replication has been called for by Tukey (1969) and Cohen (1994), among many others. Replication lowers both Type I and Type II error rates. Moreover, it is just as important as random assignment in determining what works. Reyna (p. 9) provided the definition of scientifically based research as listed in the *NCLB* legislation. The only mention of replication is that scientifically based research "includes research that (v) ensures that experimental studies are presented in sufficient detail and clarity to *allow* (emphasis added) for replication." I propose that this definition be reworded to state that scientifically based research includes experimental studies that are programmatic in nature and have been successfully replicated and extended to reliably conclude the direction and size of treatment effects and their generalizability.

Some have argued that the true experiment with random assignment may not be the best design to accomplish this. Winn (2003) proposed that design experiments may be better suited for this purpose because they are iterative, allowing the researcher to make changes in the design several times during the investigation. Winn explained that traditional experiments attempt to control too many uncontrollable variables and adapt the setting to suit the intervention, rather than adapting the intervention to suit the setting. What Winn failed to mention is that in the Fisherian tradition, true experiments are continuous, with each new experiment representing an attempt to build on the previous one. In Fisher's view, only after a treatment has been consistently shown to be reliable should we conclude that it works. Educational researchers would do well to view experiments as continuous, with the ultimate goal of strengthening internal and external validity.

One of my former mentors in grad school, Roger Bruning, has recently developed a web-based learning tool called *ThinkAboutIt*. It is designed to enhance students' critical thinking skills using technology. Rather than collect data on whether teachers and students like the tool and how they use it, which is what most of educational technology research seems to be doing these days, it would be most useful to evaluate the tool in terms of whether it does indeed enhance students' critical thinking skills. More specifically, and in line with Glass's notion of dosage-response curves, a series of studies should look at what this tool does, for whom, and under what circumstances, similar to the type of investigations that proceed when a new drug is developed and seeking FDA approval.

Instead, this culture of conducting the perfect study rather than viewing research as a process where one conducts several studies programmatically to both nail down an effect and reveal the extensions and limitations of a treatment persists. Most doctoral programs prohibit students from even beginning work on the dissertation until they apply for candidacy, usually after 2 years of coursework. Graduate students should be up to their elbows in their program of research by the time they finish their first 2 years. The dissertation should consist of a series of studies that students present at a point in time when they feel a contribution to science has been made. (This is indeed the format B. F. Skinner followed in graduate school at Harvard.) I agree with Glass that chasing the perfect study is silly. It does not exist. Rather, a series of studies that programmatically build upon each other with replications and extensions better serves science. But how do we change this culture in the face of such inertia?

RECOMMENDATIONS

The IES should tout programmatic research efforts (with replications and extensions) as loudly as they have the random assignment gold standard. Explain that a series of experiments that build upon each other to both nail down an intervention's effect and extend the effect to different learning environments and student characteristics (i.e., dosage response curves) is far preferable to meta-analyzing a set of unprogrammatic, single-shot studies that have little in common. And once a series of investigations, examined as a series, provide convincing evidence to consider implementation in schools, should we then subject the studies to a meta-analysis where we simply look at effect sizes?

Let's assume that we have a set of five programmatic experiments. The first two experiments resulted in nonsignificant p values and small effects, prompting the researchers to make some changes in the design. The third through fifth experiments result in significant p values and consistently larger effects as the researchers simply increase the length of the intervention. Because each of the five experiments investigates the efficacy of using mnemonic strategy training with fifth-graders, the meta-analyst throws the results of all five experiments into the analysis and concludes that the strategy is essentially useless, providing an average effect size that is unimpressive. What has been revealed here as opposed to concealed?

Glass (Robinson, 2004) referred to this as something Lee Cronbach called the Flat Earth Society. Averaging effect sizes is a gross misuse of meta-analysis. At minimum, exploratory data analysis techniques, including graphs, should be used (Behrens, 1997). Dosage-response curves imply looking at more than just means—researchers should dig deeper. But remember that examining a set of nonprogrammatic studies using meta-analysis holds far less potential for revealing useful information concerning which interventions work best for which students in which learning environments than does a set of programmatic studies (Wainer & Robinson, 2003). Meta-analytic techniques may serve us best when examining findings from randomized field trials (Boruch, de Moya, & Snyder, 2002).

The IES should appoint primary researchers who have conducted programmatic research to advisory posts. The technical advisory group of the What Works Clearing House is an impressive collection of mainly methodologists, several of whom would consider themselves to be meta-analysts. There is certainly nothing wrong with having methodologists provide a unique perspective on research synthesis. Reyna states that the members have "demonstrated proficiency in conducting and publishing empirical research." To provide a nice balance in the group among primary researchers and methodologists, the TAG could also use a few programmatic researchers such as Joel Levin, Rich Mayer, Alice Corkill, and so on.

Editors should start by redefining the unit size of the research article. Requiring a series of experiments that replicate and extend, rather than piecemeal, single-shot studies would allow researchers to see that research is a continuing process, not a who-can-design-the-best-study-contest.

David Mick, editor of the *Journal of Consumer Research*, recently created a section on re-inquiries that published replications of previously published studies (Mick, 2001). An excellent way for graduate students to learn the research process would be to first conduct a few of these replication studies of existing studies. As mentioned previously, Fisher expected replications when he developed significance testing. By requiring multiple-experiment studies and encouraging independent replications, editors would improve our situation.

Graduate programs should revise dissertation requirements. View the dissertation as a series of investigations rather than one impressive study. Teach statistics and research methods courses by presenting sets of studies to interpret rather than single studies. When discussing single studies, talk about what information the study provides as informing the researcher about what to do next. Do we tinker with the design? Do we increase our sample size? Do we adjust the intervention? Do we use a different age group of subjects? These are the questions that drive programmatic research.

Finally, universities should revise how they evaluate professors for promotion and tenure and merit raises. Stop counting number of publications and instead look more closely at each publication. A multiple-experiment article that actually contributes something should count more than single studies that contribute little and simply await the meta-analyst.

REFERENCES

Behrens, J. T. (1997). Principles and procedures of exploratory data analysis. *Psychological Methods, 2,* 131-160.

Boruch, R., de Moya, D., & Snyder, B. (2002). The importance of randomized field trials in education and related areas. In F. Mosteller & R. Boruch (Eds.), *Evidence matters: Randomized field trials in education research.* Washington, DC: Brookings Institution Press.

Chung, W., Acee, T., Hsieh, Y., Kim, H., Thomas, G., Hsieh, P., & Robinson, D. (2004, April). *Declines in experimental research.* Paper presented at the annual meeting of the American Educational Research Association, San Diego, CA.

Cohen, J. (1990). Things I have learned (so far). *American Psychologist, 45,* 1304–1312.

Cohen, J. (1994). The earth is round (*p* < .05). *American Psychologist, 49,* 997–1003.

Glass, G. V. (1976). Primary, seconday, and meta-analysis of research. *Educational Researcher, 5,* 3–8.

Glass, G. V. (2000). *Meta-analysis at 25.* Retrieved from http://glass.ed.asu.edu/gene/papers/meta25.html

Mick, D. G. (2001). Editorial: Announcing a new section on re-inquiries. *Journal of Consumer Research, 28*. Retrieved September 18, 2003, from http://wiscinfo. doit.wisc.edu/jcr/June2001ed.htm.

Robinson, D. H. (2004). An interview with Gene V Glass. *Educational Researcher, 33*(3), 26-30.

Robinson, D. H., Whittaker, T., Williams, N., & Beretvas, S. N. (2003). It's not effect sizes so much as comments about their magnitude that mislead readers. *Journal of Experimental Education, 72*, 51-64.

Schmidt, F. L. (1996). Statistical significance testing and cumulative knowledge in psychology: Implications for training of researchers. *Psychological Methods, 1*, 115–129.

Tukey, J. W. (1969). Analyzing data: Sanctification or detective work. *American Psychologist, 24*, 83–91.

Wainer, H., & Robinson, D. H. (2003). Shaping up the practice of null hypothesis significance testing. *Educational Researcher, 32*(7), 23-31.

Whitehurst, G. J. (2003, April). *The Institute of Education Sciences: New wine, new bottles.* Paper presented at the annual meeting of the American Educational Research Association, Chicago, IL.

Winn, W. (2003). Research methods and types of evidence for research in educational technology. *Educational Psychology Review, 15*, 367-373.

CHAPTER 12

PRUDENT INQUIRY

Conceptual Complexity versus Practical Simplicity in Knowing What Works

William R. Shadish

Reyna (this issue) has provided us with a useful service, summarizing clearly and cogently much of the history and the substance of the *No Child Left Behind Act,* and its many effects on the practice of both education and educational research. I find little to quarrel with in her excellent paper. Instead, I would like to complement her discussion of the evidence-based practice movement, based on my experience as a member of the What Works Clearinghouse Technical Advisory Group in particular, and on my more general experience as a scholar in the areas of meta-analysis, experimental design, and program evaluation.

To make my values clear at the start, I am a firm supporter of the evidence-based practice movement, and of the value of an experimenting practice and attitude in understanding what works. However, I also oppose efforts to define "good science" as "experimental science" or even as "quantitative science"(remember Einstein once said "An experiment is something everybody believes except the person who made it," Holton,

The No Child Left Behind *Legislation:*
Educational Research and Federal Funding, 129–134
Copyright © 2005 by Information Age Publishing
All rights of reproduction in any form reserved.

1986, p. 13). Rather, the balance of research methods used in any field at any given time should reflect such matters as the extant questions judged by the research and policy community to be important, the state of existing knowledge about those questions, the feasibility of mounting different kinds of studies given resource constraints, and the likelihood that answers to those questions can be provided in a timely manner and could influence either thinking or practice in the field (Shadish, Cook, & Campbell, 2002; Shadish, Cook, & Leviton, 1991). Are treatment effectiveness questions particularly salient in education? Does the educational literature already contain good answers to these questions? Does the educational community have sufficient resources and expertise to mount such studies? Would the answers to treatment effectiveness questions affect thinking or policy? These questions are likely to be at the heart of many commentaries on Reyna's article.

I will focus on one little piece of the answer to these questions—the conceptual and methodological complexity of understanding what works. Issues of treatment effectiveness have become much more salient in recent years, not just in education, but in many fields. This has manifested itself in a variety of ways, including the work of the Cochrane Collaboration in the United Kingdom, the Campbell Collaboration in the United States, and the What Works Clearinghouse. Indeed, the entire movement that is generally referred to as evidence-based practice is centrally concerned with issues of treatment effectiveness. However, along with this salience has come renewed debate about the criteria and standards that should apply in making the judgment about what works. Many of these debates trade on the existence of competing conceptual and practical demands—the trade-off between the conceptual complexity of knowing what works versus the practical necessity for simple rules that are inherent in any widespread practical enterprise like the evidence-based practice movement. Such debates often proceed as follows: The first side describes its practices in understanding what works, the second side demonstrates the conceptual inadequacies in those practices, the first side then responds with something like "Well, if you can do it better, please do so," and so on. In fact, what these exchanges illustrate is exactly my point: Finding a reasonable balance between competing conceptual and practical demands is at the heart of evidence-based practice.

Conceptually, making judgments about treatment effects benefits from an understanding of the logics of causal inference. I use the plural logics intentionally, for there exist a variety of pertinent conceptual lenses through which we understand causation, for example:

- The logic that suggests that a causal inference requires us to show that cause precedes effect, cause co-varies with effect, and alternative causes of the observed effect are implausible.
- The counterfactual model of causation that suggests that when you have a given cause, the effect is the difference on posttest between the treated participants and the counterfactual—that is, what the posttest would have been on those same participants if they had not received treatment.
- Mackie's notion of a cause as an INUS condition—"an *insufficient* but *non-redundant* part of an *unnecessary* but *sufficient* condition" (Mackie, 1974, p. 62; italics in original). Mackie's theory reminds us that what we call a cause is a complex package of conditions, including background variables we may rarely recognize explicitly, in addition to what we think of as the cause, and that identifying a cause usually requires a long program of research.
- The distinction between descriptive causation (did A cause B) and causal explanation (why did A cause B).

These four conceptual schemes only begin to illustrate the very extensive and complex conceptual literature on causation that exists across many different fields. The four schemes overlap but also contribute unique ideas. Since few treatment outcome researchers are philosophers, few of us really know all these schemes very well. That is unfortunate because saying that a treatment is effective requires making a convincing case that all these conceptual attributes of a cause are met. As a corollary, we can also see that determining what works is primarily a conceptual problem, not a methodological problem.

That being said, logic and concepts by themselves are not enough. We need data, or observations, to help us map the treatment and its putative effects back onto the concepts about causation. Hence we need designs and methodologies that provide that data pertinent to causation, including but not limited to:

- Randomized experiments
- Quasi-experiments
- Observational studies
- Surveys
- Causal modeling
- Case studies

Each of these methods can have at least some role to play in descriptive causal inference, albeit sometimes a limited one (Campbell, 1975). Few people ever master all these designs, especially in the nuances of their strengths and weaknesses in assisting causal inference. Even methodologists often have some mastery of only a few of them; and the average researcher is an expert in one at most. This introduces even more complexity into the task of assessing what works.

Another key problem is that the logics and the designs described above only map onto each other imperfectly. For example, randomized experiments do ensure that cause precedes effect; but they only rule out alternative explanations on expectation, not very well in single studies with small samples, the context in which many causal inferences are made. Similarly, randomized experiments only tell us about causal description, not causal explanation. Surveys often measure cause and effect simultaneously, making it difficult to determine whether cause preceded effect or vice versa. In both quasi-experiments and case studies, the ability of the researcher to identify all the pertinent alternative explanations is often modest. All this introduces still more complexity.

So it is clear that making statements about what works can be a very complex matter, requiring knowledge of complex concepts, of many different kinds of methods, and of the complex matches and mismatches between designs, data, and concepts. Not very many people have all this expertise.

All this complexity poses a dilemma, then, for practical enterprises like the What Works Clearinghouse, the Cochrane Collaboration, and the Campbell Collaboration. Doing the best possible job of finding out what works requires seasoned judgment and expertise in a variety of conceptual and methodological matters. But widespread practical enterprises like the evidence-based practice movement have few people with that expertise. Hence such enterprises require relatively simple rules that can be accurately and reliably coded at a low level of inference. This has led nearly all these enterprises to adopt some simple hierarchies such as:

- Level 1: Reviews consisting of only randomized experiments
- Level 2: Reviews consisting of both randomized and nonrandomized experiments.
- Level 3: Reviews consisting of only quasi-experiments

Some of these hierarchies add distinctions such as that between randomized experiments with and without attrition, or quasi-experiments with and without matching (though the justification for such distinctions is considerably more difficult than that for random assignment). Nearly all of them encourage researchers to explore the effects of other methodological variables such as masking to conditions, dependent variable reactivity, or kind of control group used. However they are formulated, such hierarchies are efforts to generate satisfactory answers about what works, but we can see that their very simplicity glosses over the complexities of the task, at least to some degree.

Cutting across all this is another problem, one of technology. Evidence based practice has evolved to become largely a synthesis movement in which sets of studies about a treatment are cumulated into a systematic review, often culminating in a meta-analysis. That means that such enterprises are limited by the available technologies for doing such reviews, and by the number of people trained to use those technologies. Most of those technologies are well-developed only for a few kinds of designs, mostly randomized and nonrandomized experiments. Most people trained to do such syntheses are trained in these latter methods. We do not have as well-developed technologies for integrating other kinds of designs such as case studies or single-case time series designs, and even fewer people who are trained in the use of those technologies.

So, I hope I have impressed my readers with the complexity of standard setting for making inferences about what works. To borrow terminology from Herbert Simon (1997), I think the best we can hope for is satisfycing rather than optimizing solutions, that is, systems for doing such syntheses that reach a satisfaction threshold that we all recognize is not optimal, but that is viewed by many stakeholders as good enough. However, no system will ever be viewed as good enough by all stakeholders. Consequently, we need to encourage multiple and diverse systems so we can learn about their strengths and weaknesses by experience. This will allow us to develop the data-based criticisms of the results of these systems. The Campbell Collaboration, for example, is using existing meta-analytic technologies that can be practically implemented on a wide scale, based on some relatively simple rules for the kinds of methods that can be combined. However, that organization is simultaneously encouraging some of its interested members to develop methods for the use of process and qualitative data in the research synthesis process. As the latter methods become better developed, more researchers will be trained in them, and they can take their place in the mix.

However, it is incumbent on those of us who may have the requisite expertise to, on the one hand, support all these practical efforts as good faith efforts to produce satisfycing solutions while, on the other hand, pointing to the potential pitfalls that that our experience leads us to expect these efforts to suffer from, both generically and in the specifics. For example:

- Can systematic reviews distinguish between treatments that do not work vs treatments that were not implemented properly or at all?

- Do we have the requisite empirical knowledge about research methodology to make the kinds of judgments that some of these systems ask us to make (e.g., how much attrition is too much attrition in a randomized experiment)?
- Are we likely to overlook important unintended side effects that may not have been measured in an experiment, but might have been noted by qualitative methodologies?
- Can such reviews cogently address questions of scale that inevitably arise when generalizing from a set of local experiments to broad policy implementation on a state or national scale?

These are just some of the pressing questions that will continue to emerge as we learn more about methods for doing evidence-based practice.

All these complexities remind me of one of my favorite quotes, this one by Shapin (1994) from his book on the tensions between the social and epistemological approaches to truth. He said, "prudence sat poised between skepticism and credulity" (Shapin, 1994, p. xxix). That should be our motto. Our aim is not just truth nor is it just skepticism. Our aim is prudent inquiry.

REFERENCES

Campbell, D. T. (1975). "Degrees of freedom" and the case study. *Comparative Political Studies, 8*, 178-193.

Holton, G. (1986). *The advancement of science, and its burdens.* Cambridge, England: Cambridge University Press.

Mackie, J. L. (1974). *The cement of the universe: A study of causation.* Oxford, England: Oxford University Press.

Simon H. (1997). *Models of bounded rationality, Vol. 3. Empirically grounded economic reason.* Cambridge, MA: MIT Press.

Shadish, W. R., Cook, T. D., & Campbell, D. T. (2002). *Experimental and quasi-experimental designs for generalized causal inference.* Boston: Houghton-Mifflin.

Shadish, W. R., Cook, T. D., & Leviton, L. C. (1991). *Foundations of program evaluation: Theories of practice.* Newbury Park, CA: Sage.

Shapin, S. (1994). *A social history of truth: Civility and science in seventeenth-century England.* Chicago: The University of Chicago Press.

CHAPTER 13

FEDERAL POLICY AND SCIENTIFIC RESEARCH

Valerie F. Reyna

It was an honor to be associated with, in the words of Professor Phye, "two of the most important education mandates enacted in the last 25 years" (p. 103), passed with broad bipartisan support. I appreciate the opportunity to clarify and expand on my overview of federal policy, scientific research, and the emerging field of educational sciences. The thoughtful comments of this distinguished group of scholars outline the issues that will emerge in educational research and policy in the decades to come. I cannot do justice to the many important ideas expressed in these commentaries, and so I urge readers to consult them in detail. They bear reading and re-reading.

At a global level, I would characterize these commentaries as in remarkable agreement with the substance of my arguments. Some commentators express unalloyed enthusiasm and augment the arguments, while others essentially maintain that the arguments are sound (or at least not worth challenging) but that there are crucial qualifications and additional issues that merit attention. A few commentators, representing the views of many others in the field, are in agreement about major points but

The No Child Left Behind *Legislation:*
Educational Research and Federal Funding, 135–150
Copyright © 2005 by Information Age Publishing
All rights of reproduction in any form reserved.

they remain ambivalent about whether data should rule over belief and are otherwise diffusely irritated. Rather than reiterate points of agreement, I will focus mainly on those comments that diverge from or go beyond my own. The rejoinder is organized into four sections, which range from ensuring the supply of sound research that supports specific educational practices to ensuring the outcome of such practices through testing and accountability.

ENSURING THE SUPPLY OF SOUND RESEARCH TO SUPPORT EDUCATIONAL PRACTICE

Robinson makes the point that recent trends in publications are more extreme than one might have imagined: Articles that report results of educational interventions using experimental designs have virtually disappeared from some major educational journals and, for others, have dwindled precipitously in the short period from 1995 to 2002. Calfee (p. 50) agrees that, "a review by professional organizations of publication trends might indeed be useful for informing policy." As I discussed in my chapter, experiments are only one of many acceptable designs in scientific research. Thus, Allington's (p. 38) claim that "assertions are unscientific because there have been no randomized experiments testing their accuracy" directly contradicts what I said in my chapter. Although Allington is correct that correlational data are used (along with experiments and other forms of data) to inform medical guidelines, the evidence is not considered interchangeable with experiments with respect to the specific question of causation. Such evidence is often explicitly graded in quality with respect to the question of causation (e.g., in the congestive heart failure guidelines of the Agency for Health Care Policy and Research). Allington also recounts shortcomings in medicine in which not all drugs have been tested in all populations, all practitioners do not read the primary research literature and apply it in their clinical practice, practice does not necessarily follow evidence-based guidelines, and hospitals and others are gaming the system to avoid being held accountable for outcomes. I agree that these are bad things to do (I have in fact published on some of these issues, such as practice deviation from medical guidelines), and that educational practitioners should not emulate them, per my chapter. Allington (p. 39) calls this a case of "the pot calling the kettle black," but I would characterize it as two wrongs do not make a right. The crucial difference between medicine and education, however, is not that one field is perfect, but that there is a broad consensus in medicine that these are bad things to do, that it is a criticism rather than a virtue to say that a common practice is based only on professional intuition.

Shadish enumerates five scientific designs and methodologies in addition to randomized experiments that are pertinent to causation. The problem with the trend in educational research, however, is that education is a pragmatic enterprise; the goals of education are (at a minimum) to teach content, thinking, and skills and only experiments yield conclusive information about which practices promote these goals (Reyna, 2004). Contrary to Calfee's comments about hormone replacement therapy, it is precisely because previous evidence was based on correlational data, and not on randomized control trials, that the more recent, superior design yielded different results.

Shadish points out that experiments are not informative if they are poorly executed, and problems such as attrition (especially differential attrition from treatment and control groups) raise complex issues, such as how much attrition is too much. He also raises pragmatic issues, such as policy needs and the supply of trained quantitative analysts. As for the observation that most professionals do not have expertise in all methodologies, I would suggest the tried-and-true method of collaboration. However, Shadish is correct that the supply of trained methodologists must be increased appreciably to meet national needs. I disagree, however, that we need to encourage multiple and diverse systems for synthesizing results simply to gain experience; we should continue to seek best practices for syntheses based on available knowledge and not waste resources and produce misleading conclusions in the interest of variety. For example, the efforts to synthesize case histories and qualitative studies seem odd considering that those methodologies are about rich descriptions of individuals or unique cases, and inferences about groups would be logically unsound in any event.

One might justify descriptive or correlational research (that was related to theories about effectiveness of educational practices) if there were a need to generate hypotheses as opposed to test them. In the context of deciding what is effective, the logical progression is from exploratory descriptive and preliminary correlational studies that generate possibilities to experiments that eliminate possibilities (see also Levin & O'Donnell's, 1999, stage model). Thus, the trend of decreasing experimentation and increasing (inconclusive) exploration does not make sense—unless one believes that there is a paucity of opinions or hypotheses about education. I know of no one on any side of this issue who thinks that we do not have many hypotheses about educational effectiveness that seem to be repeatedly recycled rather than thoroughly tested—and testing hypotheses would eliminate some of them and produce actual progress.

Robinson makes many additional interesting arguments about postmodernism, meta-analysis, significance, effect sizes, and graduate study. For example, he argues that the definition of scientific research ought to include studies that are programmatic, have been replicated, and whose effect sizes can be estimated and generalized. (He cautions about averaging effect sizes when studies are not comparable.) O'Donnell points up the need to gather data about how effect sizes vary in different contexts, and wonders whether we might discover that "effects of particular programs, instructional strategies, or curricula were not attainable in certain contexts." Effect sizes and variability in context are empirical questions, as in all fields; the scientific method is the process for achieving the goals of reliability and replicability. These are laudable goals for research that go beyond basic definitions to desiderata, and are the sorts of standards used in, for example, applying results of clinical trials in the practice of medicine. As more solid research evidence accumulates, I predict that these standards will ultimately prevail in education. This badly needed research will be supplied more rapidly if graduate students are "up to their elbows" in research as soon as possible in their graduate study—as they are in other scientific fields. Including more than one study in dissertations, publishing articles that report results of several related studies, and replicating earlier studies as part of follow-up studies that refine and extend hypotheses, are also standard practice in other scientific fields and should become so in education.

Hunt's comments about confusing the essence of science with its surface aspects, such as peer review, are well taken. He is right. However, the physicist he described works in a field with mountains of highly precise data and specific mathematical formulae that make precise predictions. Those background facts were probably well known to this physicist and so he did have an alternative model, the current one, that did not include the anomaly (i.e., the small number of pulsars that behaved in an anomalous way). In this highly constrained arena, deviation in the form of a precise and testable hypothesis (after all, the equations might not have fit the data, which was a test of the hypothesis) is justifiable. Nothing like this constrained state of affairs exists in education. Peer review is not the scientific method, it is only a process for judging it; nor is it infallible. If a qualified educator could glean enough methodological information from non-peer-reviewed sources, and the data were adequately analyzed and interpreted, the strength of the evidence is what should count. However, who is to judge the strength of the evidence (note that I said a "qualified" educator who would, therefore, be a peer)? That judgment is not a matter of expert *opinion*, which has characterized some previous efforts to judge research quality, but involves applying consistent scientific standards (see Shadish's commentary for some of those standards and O'Donnell's commentary for descriptions of earlier efforts). In the main, peer review by qualified reviewers accomplishes this task of judging evidence strength. However, like democracy, it is a flawed system that does not guarantee infallibility. The *No Child Left Behind* legislation provides needed specificity in a field that does not have a tradition of scientific peer review, one that is based on "observation as the arbiter of truth, rather than relying on appeals to personal belief, faith, or ideology."

Robinson makes a number of structural suggestions to ensure the supply of necessary research, the most significant of which in my view is the call for a formal role for experienced researchers as advisors to the Institute of Education Sciences (IES). To be sure, the IES regularly solicits information from scientists, for example, as part of peer review or panel discussions and has an advisory board that includes scientists. However, a secure and mature organization should welcome advice from scientists with a track record of empirical research in key areas, such as reading comprehension, mathematics learning, and scientific problem solving. Experienced researchers should also fill the higher echelons of managerial and supervisory positions in the IES, as well as some other positions, consistent with the recommendations of the National Academy of Sciences. Regrettably, IES seems to be having difficulty attracting and retaining researchers of any level of experience for positions within the organization and upper-level positions are not necessarily filled by researchers or even doctoral level professionals. Other federal research agencies also find it difficult to hire enough professionals with research experience, especially into permanent positions, and so the problem is not unique to IES. Despite the intelligence, hard work, and accomplishments of federal employees who are not researchers at IES, there is no substitute for research experience throughout the organization in order to have the most basic insights into research generation and evaluation, as concluded by the National Academy of Sciences and alluded to in the Education Sciences Reform Act of 2002. Solving the problem of attracting qualified researchers to leadership positions will be an important performance measure for IES, and will make the difference in whether current accomplishments are only a temporary educational fad or are sustained beyond the tenure of individuals.

WHAT KIND OF RESEARCH IS NEEDED?

Phye's elegant essay makes a number of good points that need not be repeated, so I will select only a few items for comment. Phye agrees that the view from the heartland is essentially the same as that from Washington. However, he underlines the importance of valid theory, emphasizing not only what works but how it works, i.e., the processes through which learning is achieved. Shadish (p. 131) similarly distinguishes between "descriptive causation (did A cause B) and causal explanation (why did A cause B)." Calfee (p. 53) describes data about "theories of intervening mechanisms" as more convincing than other kinds of data. Mitchell (p. 91) points out a historical fact that used to be an assumption underlying federal budget discussions, but seems to be elusive today: "Even within the history of scientific medicine, the most important advances were the result of research work leading to dramatic reorganizations in thinking about disease, not just in the verification of the efficacy of specific treatments." In other words, research that focuses on causal mechanisms is essential even if our goals are only practical ones (i.e., if there were no benefit to advancing knowledge for its own sake).

Phye (p. 108) further distinguishes competency theory and performance theory, drawing on psycholinguistics: "Competency models can be logically developed at a philosophical level of analysis without direct observation or empirical testing." Performance models, in contrast, "require direct observation." Although I share Phye's emphasis on theory, I recall the competency-performance distinction somewhat differently. Competence is underlying ability; performance is what is observed. For example, children might be able to point to the right answer (the more likely option) in a probability judgment task but not be able to explain it verbally because they lack the correct vocabulary. Or, to take a simpler example, testing people under noisy, hot conditions would underestimate their competence; performance would be interfered with by extraneous conditions that are immaterial to real competence. In this view, competence and performance are both derivable from data, but competence is analogous to unobservable constructs that are, nevertheless, crucially supported by inferences from observable evidence.

Phye (p. 110) argues that "it is the human memory metaphor that puts the learner at the center of the research process when attempting to address academic learning issues," in contrast to current educational research. Hunt concurs that research on cognition, development, and individual differences are relevant to education (though I reiterate my mention of areas outside of psychology, such as economics, the natural and physical sciences, and other fields). However, Hunt (p. 67) is concerned about the evolution of psychology in the direction of neuroscience, which he worries (with Bruer, 2003) may be "a bridge too far" to education. Hunt is correct that psychology's rush to neuroscience will inhibit its relevance to behavioral fields such as education—unless IES and other educational research agencies sustain the relevant behavioral work. The Cognition and Student Learning program of IES already funds relevant neuroscientific research on learning. Indeed, basic research on learning is the source of new ideas and is where the future breakthroughs in educational practice will come from. The need for basic understanding is greater in education, according to Mitchell (p. 91), because our grasp of the "basic mechanisms of action" is weaker, compared to medicine or physics. As Mitchell (p. 91) concludes, "productive research requires more than reliable and valid techniques of data collection and analysis, it also requires a sound theoretical grasp of the underlying mechanisms at work in the domain of study."

AFTER RESEARCH, THEN WHAT?
ENGINEERING RESEARCH INTO PRACTICE

Hunt presents qualifications to my arguments and to assumptions in the Education acts. He makes the sensible point that the availability of sound scientific research does not guarantee a successful educational system: Educational engineering is needed to take advantage of these advances and ensure their effective implementation. I wholeheartedly agree with O'Donnell (p. 100) that, "problems of implementation are significant and have important effects on the morale of school personnel." Mitchell makes similar points, and emphasizes the need to train school personnel so that they understand interventions; Allington mentions the important role of teacher autonomy in feeling accountable. According to Lyon (p. 85), "there continues to be an alarming paucity of knowledge about how best to implement trustworthy research findings in complex environments such as schools and classrooms."

In response to Calfee, I acknowledge as I did in my chapter, that there were laudable efforts to translate research into practice before the recent changes (and history should be studied). I would quibble with Hunt (p. 59) about whether previous educational research efforts at the federal level were consistently marked by "good scientific reasoning," despite good intentions and many positive features. Contrary to Calfee's comparison, the What Works Clearinghouse is not similar in kind to ERIC, which makes available often unpublished and unreviewed research (fulfilling a useful but different function). However, Hunt's main thesis is correct that education continues as usual as if projects with demonstrated results never existed. Hunt offers the model of the Department of Defense, which sponsors research all along the continuum from basic to applied, including translational research that is aimed at accomplishing the goal of transferring knowledge from the laboratory to the field. There are other successful examples of translational research as well, such as the National Cancer Institute, which sponsors research ranging from the laboratory bench to the patient's bedside. Supporting sufficient learning research that provides a bridge to the classroom is necessary and overdue.

Hunt describes a familiar sequence of events: the funded and supported research project with trained staff and then the subsequent implementation without special funding and support. He concludes that money would facilitate implementation, and he could be right, but it still might not be faithful implementation because of the lack of training of school personnel in the logic of standardization of treatment. However, the Federal Drug Administration does not take lack of money as an excuse for deviating from policies requiring proof of safety and effectiveness of drugs. When orange juice cartons displayed claims that were not supported by scientific evidence, the government (probably at some cost to the company) summarily confiscated them. When doctors want to deviate substantially from standards of evidence-based practice, the system does not enable that behavior (e.g., insurance companies will refuse to pay doctors for treatments that lack evidence of effectiveness). Doctors are not given an incentive to provide scientifically supported care; they are expected to provide such care or risk charges of malpractice. The latter is the logic of *No Child Left Behind*, although the sanctions are not as harsh as they are in medicine. The sanctions include shutting down schools, removing leadership, and reassigning teachers.

Among the practical impediments Hunt cites is cost. The decision to adopt a new program, policy, or practice in many fields is driven not only by evidence of effectiveness but also by considerations of cost (as in cost effectiveness). Polls consistently show that Americans support education, and would be willing to invest more if they could see a return on that investment. Until there is evidence that current investments are being well managed, there will be a reluctance to invest more. Experimentation on a large scale and in the field should not be taken lightly, but, as Hunt indicates, is an essential part of research and development. The suggestion is not to wildly select any crazy program and experiment with it, but rather, to select realistic alternatives such as current approaches to algebra instruction compared to an alternative method that has good initial evidence (i.e., good phase I and II trial results as in medical clinical trials). Calfee advocates a similar system of gathering preliminary evidence in small-scale settings before pursuing large-scale clinical trials comparing alternative programs. It is difficult for me to see how this kind of experimentation would not be vastly superior to current practice to which students are subjected, mostly without any evidence to support it. Field research is conducted in busy, real-world environments such as hospitals every day using rigorous randomized experimental designs and without much loss of generality (although patients may be more uniform than they are in ordinary clinical practice and lack co-morbidities).

AFTER RESEARCH-BASED PRACTICES ARE IMPLEMENTED: TESTING AND ACCOUNTABILITY

Hunt's (p. 58) characterization of American educational achievement in the elementary years (i.e., "American schools do pretty well" in the early years and that difficulties ensue in middle and high school) is not accurate based on national assessments, as Lyon's commentary aptly describes. Data from the National Assessment of Educational Progress, for example, indicates that only 31 percent of fourth-graders were proficient at reading, a basic skill, as of 2003. Calfee (p. 49) notes that reading achievement has "improved somewhat in recent decades" and "mathematics even more," but he does not say that the level of achievement is acceptable.

Drawing on his knowledge of research and policy, including the history of earlier attempts, Lyon explains the need and rationale for *No Child Left Behind*, with specific examples describing the evolution of research-based reading programs. He argues with compelling clarity that educational policies and practices were unlikely to change without linking funding to accountability for results. This view contrasts sharply with Pressley's impression that educational research already shapes classroom practices. On closer examination, there is no real contradiction here, or with the observations I make that are in line with Lyon's. I grant that educational research has sometimes in some classrooms affected educational practices, including the ones cited by Pressley. However, the fact remains that most educational practice is not based on sound scientific research, and Pressley does not address that claim. As Lyon eloquently recounts, until recently there has been no well-established conduit or set of procedures to systematically transfer research findings into the classroom. Lyon provides details of such procedures, a blueprint for appropriately monitored implementation of research-based programs at the state level.

Lyon (p. 79) also indicates that there are barriers to acceptance of scientifically supported practices were they to be made available to schools, among these "a decided antiscientific spirit within the education profession." In places, Pressley's commentary exemplifies this antiscientific spirit, but paradoxically a conflicted high regard for the scientific approach. To take but a few examples of the former: "I chuckle as I contemplate the possibility of evidence-based, educational programs being subjected to fully randomized experimental trials" (p. 114) or "Those making this point mutter something about multiple field-based, experimental trials and medical research as they sermonize" (p. 116). These kinds of remarks fail to speak to the issues; instead, they describe people with different views from Pressley's in *ad hominem* terms. Pressley's comments are not extreme on this dimension, but they unfortunately illustrate what is all too often the tenor of the educational "debate." Calfee

(p. 55) provides additional examples, such as using the term "privilege" as in "the shifting of research funds to privilege certain forms of research (and certain researchers)" as though specific individuals ("certain researchers") had an unfair advantage that was the result of "privilege" rather than *earning* high marks for research from peer reviewers applying the same rigorous standards evenhandedly to everyone. The scientific approach eschews this kind of non-argument. It is not that scientists never think such things or are too superior to express them; it is simply a question of commitment to the principle that evidence is what matters. Pressley and Calfee have been paragons of the scientific approach, and their leadership is needed at this crucial time in our nation's history. If there was any lack of clarity in my chapter about this point, let me clarify it now: Standards of scientific rigor must be evenhandedly applied to all, regardless of who they are and what discipline they come from. Furthermore, the mandate for minimum standards of scientific rigor is not unfunded; it is connected, in principle if not in fact, to every dollar spent on education.

Hunt provides an important distinction between using assessment to gauge minimum performance versus using it to provide constructive feedback to improve education. O'Donnell seems to be suggesting a third possibility, that consequences that accrue to schools will be reflected in test scores. O'Donnell reports that Viadero (2003) found no such evidence of academic gains associated with high-stakes testing. As no methodological information is given, it is not clear whether or how Viadero tested this hypothesis. Therefore, it is impossible to know whether these conclusions are supported by the data. (As a matter of routine, conclusions from empirical studies should be accompanied by a brief description of the design, methods, including participants and measures, and how data were analyzed.) Again, summative (as well as formative) assessment is important: No one expects HIV tests to cure AIDS, but information about the incidence and prevalence of infection is used to develop policies and treatments.

As Hunt indicates, test results would have to be rapidly fed back to teachers in classrooms in an understandable format to achieve the improvement goal. Alexander and Riconscente make a similar point. As Hunt indicates, software is available today that will accomplish that goal, but the D (for development) in R & D has been relatively ignored (I am intentionally ignoring those programs that have D without the necessary R). As objective methods for assessment are put in place across the nation, and as they continue to be improved (which is the norm for science), schools that were considered successful based on subjective grounds may indeed be found to be unsuccessful (and vice versa); that is no justification for failing to assess schools properly. Parents and school officials should ask questions when professionals give inconsistent feedback, but they should demand honest assessments and improved methods, not politically manufactured "success." I am not commenting about the particular example of the school given by O'Donnell nor about its assessment and re-assessment, because she gives no information relevant to which assessment was the valid one.

Alexander and Riconscente (p. 28) correctly note that "learning is much broader than achievement of basic skills in threshold domains," a point that I tried to convey. "Strategic processing," for example, was on the list I provided, and is what I would consider to be part of learning and cognition. There are people who believe that only basic skills are important, but I have never been one of them and my chapter explicitly mentions higher-order cognition and metacognition as essential aspects of student learning. As Mitchell stresses, affective and motivational factors are also important elements of learning. Alexander and Riconscente also make the excellent point that basic skills instruction need not occur prior to instruction in higher-order thinking skills, and such practice would be inconsistent with research. Moreover, I would encourage Alexander, Riconscente, and likeminded others to champion or develop valid assessments (i.e., tests) of higher-order cognition that could be routinely included in student achievement tests. Ideal tests will assess higher-order cognition as well as basic threshold skills, and will assess transfer of knowledge rather than memorization of specific test items (e.g., Wolfe, Reyna, & Brainerd, in press). Alexander and Riconscente remind us that teaching to the test is a bad thing if the motivation is purely extrinsic, as contrasted with learning for its own sake that is intrinsically reinforcing. As I discussed in my chapter, the goal of teaching is learning (in the broad sense of that term) and performance on a test will reflect learning if that test is valid, but it is not an end in itself.

Alexander and Riconscente (p. 31) make a number of comments about "current educational rhetoric and policies" that do not apply to my chapter, and that do not seem to apply to programs and policies such as *No Child Left Behind* either. For the sake of clarity, I should reiterate: I know of no one who seriously claims that instruction will eliminate all individual differences, and this is not a goal of *No Child Left Behind*. Instead, the goal is, in the words of Alexander and Riconscente (p. 31), "every student deserves the opportunity to succeed to the best of his or her abilities." The ideal is that all students will read at grade level—as a *minimum* and within reason as there are exceptions in the legislation for profoundly handicapped children. I cannot imagine anyone seriously arguing that students should be held back to lower levels of achievement if they exceed the average. Hence, Alexander and Riconscente (p. 32) need not be concerned about any "devastating" "loss of human potential."

In addition, in the happy event that all students were to achieve a minimum of performance at grade level, there is no reason why "we would have to move the bar higher" (p. 31) unless there were some good reason to do so. I am not sure what the implication is of the statement that "it is the student not the classroom or school that learns well or poorly" (p. 32). Would Alexander and Riconscente keep a school open in which, say, only one student were succeeding? Schools are made up of classes, and classes are made of students, and failure can occur broadly across most (not 100%) of a school or locally within classes or even more locally for individual students. The solution to a problem should be appropriate to the scope of the problem. If one student has a problem, that student should be helped individually. If most students in a school have a problem, then a broader solution is required. Alexander and Riconscente's point about learners does not seem to encompass the fact that individual learners make up the larger units. I did not suggest, and I know of no one who has, that we should necessarily be "administering invasive emergency treatments to entire populations" regardless of the number of asymptomatic or academically "healthy" students (p. 32). However, if academic failure is broader than a few individuals, and averages for the entire school fall below a minimum, then steps need to be taken even if a few students are fine. Alexander and Riconscente's (p. 33) comments about "one-size-fits-all" paradigms also seem to have little to do with what I said in my chapter. As I did say in my chapter, programs such as *Success for All* are not presented "without qualifications." The title is an *ideal* and detailed data on variability have been consistently presented. My chapter was not about specific learning effects or interactions with contexts or populations, so neither the nomothetic nor idiographic data were discussed in detail but both levels of analysis were acknowledged. Contary to Calfee (p. 52), interactions do not "threaten the interpretive validity of an investigation;" they are often the focus of interpretation. Allington provides a number of instructive examples of interactions in medicine and education, which are standard fare in scientific research.

Pressley points out the long timelines to evaluate the results of comprehensive curricula properly and that market cycles would outpace research on outcomes if it were conducted—so we might as well give up. The timelines Pressley cites apply to many other areas of practical research (e.g., as members of the Society for Prevention Research could point out), and with many investigations going on, some results are obtained now and others are obtained later, but outcomes research is still conducted. The market cycle is similarly immaterial: Outcomes research remains essential and must be conducted. Once such research is widespread and widely promulgated, it should become a factor in the market. When the results for hormone replacement therapy from the Women's Health Initiative were released, millions of women changed their health practices, despite a large market for hormone replacement therapy. If similarly dramatic results of large trials for education practices were released, it is plausible that the educational market would also respond.

Robinson criticizes "customer satisfaction" surveys (e.g., measuring whether patients feel satisfied as opposed to medical outcomes or whether college students think that they have learned something as opposed to performance in subsequent related courses), which are misused in many areas of practical importance. As Pressley (p. 117) no doubt realizes, although "the teachers are always convinced that reading is better" in his personal experience with transactional strategies instruction, there are many practices that teachers and other professionals have believed in that have turned out to be misguided. As I have said elsewhere (e.g., Reyna, 2004), some evidence is far better than none (e.g., one experiment and correlational data). However, Robinson's (p. 125) point should be underscored: Research has repeatedly demonstrated that whether teachers and students "like" an educational practice is not the same thing as whether the students have learned. Liking is not irrelevant or unimportant, but it is not the same thing as learning.

As for human subjects protection legislation, the analogy to medical research (and the application of ill-fitting medical research constraints) antedated recent efforts to align standards for educational practice with those for medical practice. Some concerns expressed to me by members of Congress were directly aimed at perceived intrusions into privacy in educational research that would not be present in, say, research on a drug for heart disease. In that connection, it is crucial that I correct a misapprehension about my chapter discussed by Calfee (p. 53): I did not say nor did I suggest that "informed voluntary consent and confidentiality" "might be the undoing of the progress toward science enshrined in *NCLB* [*No Child Left Behind*]." On the contrary, I said "regulations under consideration at this time may present an unreasonable burden to researchers" (p. 22). These regulations would go far beyond informed voluntary consent and confidentiality. I strongly support "informed voluntary consent and confidentiality." As I stated in my chapter, "current practice in most behavioral science research that is confidential and anonymous does not place subjects at greater risk than normal activities of living" (p. 22). In other words, informed voluntary consent and confidentiality lower risks in research.

Hunt makes some excellent points about educational research risk being low in general compared to medical research, whereas there is a compulsory aspect to school attendance that is not present for medical treatment (patients can opt out of treatment). Thus, he argues, there is a duty to conduct research to improve the system because students are compelled to be exposed to it. Hunt is also right that Institutional Review Boards have no incentive, let alone a mandate, to ensure that necessary research gets done—that good things get done as opposed to bad things not getting done. The complaint is heard across the nation at many different universities that the purview of these committees is steadily growing to ever more ridiculous proportions, beyond federal law, and without oversight or checks and balances. Having been on the federal side of the desk and involved in human subjects policies, I am not sure I wholly agree but it is apparent that enormous costs are being incurred (with reductions in research productivity essential to the nation's economic well-being) without enhancing human subjects protection.

UNANSWERED QUESTIONS

O'Donnell's trenchant analysis raises several important questions that await further developments in the field. As she indicates, there needs to be more analysis of the research base for instructional strategies, which is a responsibility of all researchers not just of the government's What Works Clearinghouse. Moreover, the lack of government-sponsored reviews on every question is no reason to suspend scientific standards for practice. Rejecting or delaying the imposition of scientific standards only serves to prolong the status quo of inadequate evidence. Allington's observation that federally sponsored programs in the past have failed does not support his inference that different programs with different practices will fail in the future, especially when past programs were not broadly or faithfully implemented. Although we certainly will not gather the needed evidence if we give up and focus on what might not work, we at least create the possibility of success if we move forward and gather scientific evidence. In the meantime, as in other fields, practitioners must rely on the best available evidence—and must sometimes rely on professional intuition if there are no data (not imperfect data, but no data at all). Unfortunately, contrary to Mitchell (p. 93), "standards of professional practice" in no way guarantee that traditional interventions have "done no harm" and, contrary to Allington (p. 44), we cannot assume that the "most effective practitioners rely more on intuition (or professional wisdom developed through experience) than on evidence produced by scientists." Laboratory data gathered under tightly controlled conditions (which *increases* the likelihood that they generalize to real-life conditions), often do transfer robustly to real-life situations and at least provide a principled basis for practice. Complex interactions among context variables, individual differences, and learning techniques are routinely studied in the laboratory—and so applications to the real world need not assume (contrary to Mitchell) simple main effects and that everything else is equal. The assumption that effects change in different contexts or with different populations is just that, an assumption, sometimes unfounded. The key is that practitioners should not feel *confident* that they have identified correct practice in the absence of sound scientific evidence, and that researchers must redouble their efforts to provide evidence in the areas of greatest need first.

O'Donnell (p. 100) identifies a major problem in how arguments are framed about the training of teachers: "Arguments about the importance of teachers' subject matter knowledge are often treated as arguments against the necessity for domain-general knowledge of pedagogy, human development, and cognition." Because it has been demonstrated empirically that important assumptions about how students learn turn out to be false, formal instruction in how students learn (which includes the elements of cognition listed in my chapter) is essential for teachers. Subject matter knowledge is vital, too, and these are not interchangeable areas of competence. As O'Donnell (p. 100) so aptly puts it, subject matter knowledge is "a necessary but insufficient condition" for being an effective teacher. Mitchell (p. 95) is concerned that educational professionals will never receive the "lengthy training" that they need. However, most of the commentators are faculty members in colleges and universities who decide curriculum for teacher training. Colleges and universities should respond to these glaring omissions in the curricula for teachers, and educators and researchers should mount the same kind of national campaign that we have seen to increase subject-matter expertise among teachers to increase training in the science of learning and cognition. Humanism should not be forgotten in teaching and learning, as O'Donnell and others remind us, and is not incompatible with a scientific approach. Thus, contrary to Mitchell (p. 90), we should not shift control of school programs and practices "away from educational professionals and into the hands of social and cognitive scientists." Rather, educational professionals who have control over school programs and practices should become social and cognitive scientists, and vice versa. This country can no longer afford the luxury of unqualified people in positions of authority; the consequences for students are too painful. As Mitchell (p. 94) suggests, the contingencies that control school personnel and bureaucrats do not seem to be the "rational goals of the organization." *No Child Left Behind* is an attempt to change those contingencies. As Calfee (p. 51) cautions, however, "the system has proven remarkably resistant to innovation."

O'Donnell (p. 101) asks perhaps the most important unanswered question: What if the legislation worked? Would scientifically based practice, a qualified teacher in every classroom, accountability for results, and the option of moving to another school if results were not achieved compensate for all of the social ills and disparities that currently plague American education and that hold back student achievement? The answer is that we really do not have a choice. Like Pascal's wager, we must go forth as though we were believers in order to test the hypothesis: If we give up, we will never know if these factors can compensate, at least in part, for disadvantage and negative social influences. If we do not give up, we may find that education can compensate to a great degree for the "other forces besides schools and teachers" that influence children. The story of the American dream is that education can compensate for many disadvantages, and it is the personal story of many Americans, including me.

REFERENCES

Bruer, J. (2003). Learning and technology: A view from cognitive science. In H. F. O'Neil & R. S. Perez (Eds.), *Technology applications in education: A learning view* (pp. 159–172). Mahwah, NJ: Lawrence Erlbaum Associates.

Levin, J. R., & O'Donnell, A. M. (1999). What to do about educational research's credibility gaps? *Issues in Education: Contributions from Educational Psychology, 5,* 177–229.

Reyna, V. F. (2004). Why scientific research? The importance of evidence in changing educational practice. In P. McCardle & V. Chhabra (Eds.), *The voice of evidence in reading research: Bringing research to classroom educators* (pp. 47-58). Baltimore: P.H. Brookes.

Wolfe, C., Reyna, V. F., & Brainerd, C. J. (in press). Fuzzy-trace theory: Implications for transfer in teaching and learning. In J. P. Mestre (Ed.), *Transfer of learning from a modern multidisiplinary perspective.* Greenwich, CT: Information Age.

Viadero, D. (2003, January 8). Report finds fault with high-stakes testing. *Education Week on the Web.* Retrieved November 25, 2003, from http://www.edweek.org

Printed in the United States
79740LV00002BB/153